The
Comprehensive
Handbook
for
SBA
LOANS

Don't take NO for An answer!

An Easy Guide to Financing and Loan Guarantees from the U.S. Small Business Administration

by Charles H. Green

Advisory Press, Inc.
5600 Roswell Road Suite 210 North
Atlanta, Georgia 30342

Charles Green
4/3/96

Library of Congress Catalog Card Number: 96-83429

ISBN 0-9651230-0-6

Printed in the United States of America

Table of Contents

This publication is intended to provide current and prospective business owners with useful information which may assist them in preparing for and obtaining an SBA guaranteed business loan. This information is general in nature and is not intended to provide specific advice for any individual or business entity. While the information contained herein should be helpful to the reader, appropriate financial, accounting, tax, or legal advice should always be sought from a competent professional engaged for any specific situation.

Illustrations

Acknowledgments

There are many people I wish to thank who were instrumental in the production of this book. Without their invaluable assistance, this project would have never been possible. My long time friend Gene McKay gave me the original idea to take consulting one step further into publication and provided encouragement and many ideas over the year to make it happen. My dear friend Ellen Kierr Stein helped me find the words to communicate this information through countless hours of painstaking review.

My business partner Victoria Denson has forgiven the enormous amount of time dedicated to this project. Friends Andrew J. Tate, CPA, and Terry Pickren, a partner with the firm Lawson, Davis and Pickren, reviewed my work for accuracy in accounting and legal references. Tom Abernathy responded to my requests for help and provided very important support. John Pensinger contributed an enormous wealth of production experience.

Ron Tetenbaum generously allowed me to reproduce documents from his software program T-Soft®. His software is the best thing to happen to SBA lenders since the secondary market. The National Association of Government Guaranteed Lenders (NAGGL) provided answers to many questions or directed me to persons at the SBA Central Office who had the answer. Tony Wilkenson deserves so much credit for fostering resources of the many SBA participants to insure the future of the program.

And finally I thank my Dad, who taught me how to count money and the value of entrepreneurship.

For my wonderful children,

Gordon and Meredith

Introduction

According to the 1995 White House Conference on Small Business, 99.7% of all business entities in the United States are small businesses. These businesses represent 54% of the private work force, 52% of all commercial sales, and 50% of the private sector output.

Yet obtaining capital financing continues to be a challenge for most small businesses. With the advent of stringent banking regulations, the consolidation of major banking companies, and the prospect of interstate banking, the situation for small businesses does not promise to improve.

Many small businesses are inadequately served by lenders who fail to understand the dynamics involved in a small commercial enterprise. Loan officers are often required to handle too many responsibilities such as making consumer loans or selling Chamber of Commerce memberships. Small business lenders should be focused on the attributes of the market they serve, working to understand the broad range of traditional industries and the expanding list of new business entities.

Obtaining credit is an artful skill. If learned and applied, this skill will reward the borrower's efforts by maximizing the financing available to the company, regardless of past problems or future uncertainties. Borrowing money is successful when the applicant learns the dynamics of the lender's decision-making process.

There are many important attributes helpful to obtain financing, but none is more important to success than perseverance. A friend of mine sought to borrow funds to construct a personal care home he intended to operate. He was experienced in mortgage banking and knew the process of borrowing money. However, he had marginal equity to invest in a start-up business and he planned to be his own general contractor. He finally overcame these obstacles and got a loan approved - from the sixtieth lender he approached. That is perseverance!

Most of the books I have reviewed on this topic were written by professional writers, accountants, business consultants, and even educators. Although these books contain valid information about lending and the SBA, they were obviously not based on first-hand experience. My understanding is based on my experience as a former bank loan officer, an independent commercial loan originator, and also as a borrower. This book is written in order to share what I have learned in originating, underwriting, and servicing small business loans, particularly loans guaranteed by the U.S. Small Business Administration.

Crucial information about financing small businesses has to be researched in such diverse places as construction sites, factories, power plants, automotive shops, convenience stores, archeological sites, truck terminals, restaurant kitchens, day care centers, retail stores, insurance agencies, machine shops, equipment liquidation auctions, bankruptcy court, and even the courthouse steps on foreclosure day. These are the kind of places where small business experiences unfold.

There are important lessons to be learned on both sides of the loan transaction and unfortunately most loan officers only get to see it from behind their desk. Loan officers whose experiences have not visited these venues may have limited their capabilities to recognize the upside potential and the downside risks of a small business. This perspective cannot be learned over a lunch table.

The term "lender" is used in lieu of "bank" in recognition of the emergence of many non-bank finance companies or Small Business Lending Companies (SBLCs) which have played an important role in the delivery of SBA loans to small businesses. These non-bank companies hold a limited number of licenses to make SBA guaranteed loans issued by the agency several years ago. While new licenses are no longer issued, the SBLCs provide a major percentage of new SBA guaranteed loans.

This book provides a comprehensive study of how a qualified borrower can successfully prepare for, apply for, and obtain a business loan. Because this process is very time-consuming and costly, I recommend that any business explore the use of a competent loan consultant or "packager" to assist with the solicitation of a business loan.

Throughout the text I have attempted to communicate the information in language which can be easily deciphered by the most inexperienced entrepreneur. The book incorporates general information about many disciplines in order to describe and detail the dynamics of commercial lending. In its essence, finance can sometimes be very complex and sometimes be very simple. My goal is to collaborate with readers to provide information, direction, and expectations for the loan application process.

Chapter 1

The SBA Loan Guaranty Program

What Is the SBA?

The U.S. Small Business Administration is an agency of the federal government established in 1953 to assist small business enterprises. The most important program operated by the agency is the loan guaranty program which provides a financial guaranty to qualified, eligible businesses to enhance their ability to obtain capital financing from the private sector.

The SBA has grown steadily over the years. Since 1989, with the advent of regional bank consolidation and tougher federal banking laws, the volume of SBA guaranteed loans has more than doubled. In FY 1995, the agency guaranteed almost $8 billion in loans to over 52,000 small businesses. In the process, the agency assisted with the creation of an estimated 230,000 jobs across the United States.

Although the SBA conducts many programs to assist small businesses, the focus of this book is on the assistance provided by the 7(a) Loan Guaranty Program. This information is also applicable to the 504 Program which is administered through SBA-licensed, certified development companies.

The regulations governing these loan guaranty programs are subject to change from time to time. However, this book will provide the reader with a broad view of the regulatory and financial requirements necessary to determine eligibility and qualifications for the borrower. In addition the book will assist the reader in the efficient and effective development of a commercial loan application.

The Loan Guaranty Programs

The two primary SBA loan guaranty programs which are currently funded by Congress for small businesses are the 7(a) Loan Guaranty Program and the 504 Program. They are governed by different regulations and distinguished by: 1) eligibility standards, 2) restrictions on the use of loan proceeds, 3) repayment terms, and 4) the borrower's approval process. These two programs are described below in order for the borrower to understand what kind of funding can be obtained through the agency.

The 7(a) Program - This program is the primary loan guaranty program of the SBA. Eligible uses of the program are small business financing for acquisition or improvement of assets, refinancing existing debt, or working capital. Repayment terms are determined by the actual use of the loan proceeds:

> • *Real estate loans* can be extended for up to twenty-five years (twenty-years for refinanced real estate loans).

> • *Equipment loans* can be extended for up to ten years or to the expected useful life of the acquired equipment, whichever is shorter.

> • *Working capital loans* can be extended for up to seven years.

Lenders are guaranteed for up to 75% of the total loan amount (80% for loans under $100,000) to a maximum guaranty of $750,000. Most lenders will finance up to $1,000,000 under this program although there is no actual limit to the size of the loan.

Eligibility to participate in the 7(a) Program is limited by a measurement of either the borrower's revenues or its total number of employees as determined by the borrower's SIC (Standard Industrial Code) classification. Generally most businesses which produce no more than $5 million in total revenues or have no more than five hundred employees are eligible for SBA assistance, although the industries which are limited by the number of employees can exceed $5 million in revenues. 7(a) loans provide for full amortization of the loan with no prepayment penalties.

There are several initiative programs under the umbrella of the 7(a) Program which enable the borrower to obtain higher guarantees if the borrower qualifies. These special initiative programs are primarily intended to assist the private sector in accomplishing specific public policy objectives and involve the following borrower categories:

- *7(a) 11 Program* - This loan program is for designated areas of high unemployment or concentrations of low income individuals.

- *Veterans Loan Program* - This loan program is for Vietnam-era veterans.

- *Handicapped Assistance Loan Program* - This loan program is for business owners who have a permanent mental, physical, or emotional handicap, or for non-profit workshops operated for the benefit of handicapped individuals.

- *Contract Loan Program* - This loan program is for short-term contract financing for entrepreneurs needing temporary financing during their growth stage.

- *Solar Energy and Conservation Loan Program* - This loan program is for businesses which design, engineer, or manufacture equipment or systems to convert alternative sources of energy, provide for co-generation of energy, or increase energy efficiency.

- *Employee Trust Loan Program* - This loan program is for Employee Stock Ownership Plans (ESOPs) to finance employee-owned enterprises.

- *Pollution Control Loan Program* - This loan program is for businesses involved in the planning, design, or installation of pollution-control facilities.

- *International Trade Loan Program* - This loan program is for businesses which are pursuing international trade opportunities to accommodate their ability to engage in export sales and develop new markets for their products.

Borrowers involved in these preceding economic categories can contact the agency or their lender for more specific information about the benefits and qualifications of these initiative programs.

There are a few types of businesses which are ineligible to receive financing assistance from the SBA. In general these business activities include those based on a passive investment, those engaged solely in financing third parties, or those operating a purely speculative business activity.

Those ineligible businesses include:

- non-profit corporations
- gambling and illegal activities
- investment real property
- pyramid sales organizations
- academic schools
- speculation
- lending or investment

The 504 Program - The 504 Program was authorized by Congress to foster economic development, to create or preserve jobs, and to stimulate small business expansion. The program is offered through SBA-licensed Certified Development Companies ("CDC") which are either for-profit or non-profit financial entities responsible for processing loans under this program.

The CDCs facilitate 504 loans but are not the direct funding source for the loan proceeds. The CDCs works in conjunction with an approved SBA senior lender which provides at least half of the financing. Subordinate financing is arranged by the CDC through the issuance of SBA-guaranteed debentures.

The CDCs add another layer to the approval process for the borrower. Eligibility for the 504 Program is determined by the net income and net worth of the borrower which is usually much more flexible than the 7(a) program eligibility.

This program is structured as two loans to provide up to 90% financing for qualified real estate and capital asset financing. Construction or acquisition loans are permitted but borrowers cannot refinance existing debt under this program. The borrower is required to have a minimum 10% equity contribution. The lender provides senior financing for 50% of the transaction and the CDC provides the 40% balance with funds generated from debenture sales.

These debenture funds are obtained from public security markets. Since the debentures provide a guaranteed return to investors, the debenture portion of the 504 loans carry a prepayment penalty if paid out during the first half of the loan term. The 504 Program can provide financing up to $2,250,000 ($2,500,000 in rural areas or in situations where specific public policy objectives are achieved) and are available only on ten or twenty year terms.

Mechanics of the Program

Because the mechanics of the SBA loan guaranty program are often misunderstood there is frequent criticism of the program or dissatisfaction from the businesses which do not qualify for assistance under the program. The program is a fairly well managed endeavor of the federal government to provide needed assistance to the small business sector seeking to secure adequate capital financing.

In light of often contradictory federal banking regulations, it is doubtful that the private sector would fulfill the demand for small business financing without assistance from the SBA. The agency provides the private sector lender with a financial enhancement to permit the extension of credit which would otherwise be unavailable.

The program essentially allows the lender to apply to the agency for a guaranty for a portion of a small business loan. The agency considers this application based on a set of eligibility standards which defines the characteristics of borrowers permitted to receive this assistance. There are also some restrictions on how the proceeds of these guaranteed loans may be used.

The lender actually provides the funding for the loan and will always have direct exposure for a constant percentage of the outstanding principal balance. The lender will be the primary contact for the borrower in servicing issues.

Unless the loan is not repaid as agreed, the borrower may never be aware of the presence of the SBA after the loan closing. The borrower is not involved directly with the agency unless there is a loan default. The agency may then be required to buy the guaranteed portion of the loan from the lender and initiate collection efforts directly with the borrower.

Since the agency rarely meets the borrower or visits the business, the SBA must rely on the written application of the lender in order to approve the lender's request for a guaranty. The requirements for this application include an exhaustive set of information to insure the borrower's compliance with a myriad of financial, regulatory, and business qualifications.

These guarantees are available to small business owners, regardless of age, gender, or ethnic group. The program is governed by a rigid set of regulations which are described in a loan agreement signed by the borrower upon acceptance of the loan guaranty. Borrowers utilizing the SBA program are not more susceptible to being scrutinized by or subject to attention from any other federal agency.

Any federal or state chartered bank is capable of participating in the SBA loan guaranty programs. In addition, there are a limited number of SBA-licensed non-bank lenders which have the capability to make SBA guaranteed loans. Each lender is required to enter into a Participation Agreement (Form 750) which outlines the lender's agreement to comply with the program regulations.

These lenders have many benefits available to them through participation in the loan guaranty programs. For example, the financial guaranty permits banks to enter into lending transactions with non-credit risks which otherwise might prevent lenders from being able to accommodate the borrower. These risks might involve such criteria as the length of the loan term, the type of industry, or the type of collateral used to secure the loan.

In addition, the SBA guaranty carries the full faith and credit of the federal government enabling lenders to sell the guaranteed portions of these loans to investors and provide some liquidity to the lender's loan portfolio. This feature is particularly important to smaller community-sized banks which may have limited capital with which to expand.

The SBA loan guaranty programs are administered by over sixty district offices located throughout the country and are managed by a District Director. Supervision of the 7(a) Program is managed by the Finance Chief in each district. These districts are organized into ten regions, which are headed by a politically appointed Regional Director who are involved with broader policy issues involving the agency.

The agency operates the loan guaranty programs under a common set of rules known as Standard Operating Procedures (SOPs). In theory lenders should be able to expect uniform implementation of the SOPs throughout any region or district office in the country, but such consistency is not always the case.

Each district office has a great deal of latitude to implement the SOP and to effect policy for administering the program. Some districts are more stringent than others in the interpretation of the SOP. While these differences can lead to some frustration among lenders serving multiple markets, most borrowers are not affected beyond the restrictions of their particular district office.

Regulatory authority for the Small Business Administration and the general regulations of its business credit programs are drawn from the Code of Federal Regulations, Volume 13, Business Credit and Assistance.

Chapter 2

Dealing With a Business Lender

Putting the Process in Perspective

Borrowers are frequently frustrated with lenders who seem disinterested in considering a business loan proposal or with the lengthy amount of time required to move through the application process. Borrowers may also be indignant about the conservative approach lenders utilize to underwrite business loans. These conditions are very common and they originate from a number of factors.

Primarily, lenders are adverse to the risks. Their job is to make loan investments in situations where risk is minimized. For the risk that lenders elect to accept, they protect themselves by having several options for liquidating their investment.

In recent years bank lenders have been bogged down with an enormous amount of bureaucratic requirements to document loans. Lenders are responsible for providing a paper trail of all their decisions for eventual review by internal and external auditors and by government regulators.

In fact, the time and effort to pacify bank regulators and comply with federal banking rules have become an inproportionately large cost of doing business, interfering with the lender's capability to meet the needs of customers. The Comptroller of the Currency estimates that 14% of an average bank's operating costs are directly attributable to the cost compliance with various laws and regulations.

When lenders seem too conservative, they are responding to conditions which support their position and contribute to the borrower's frustration:

First, the lender is in business, too. The lender has a responsibility to provide a financial return for shareholders by obtaining funds from depositors or investors and then prudently lending these funds to responsible borrowers.

Lenders must contend with the continually changing cost of funds and competition from other regulated and non-regulated financial institutions. They must also produce a motivated and competent labor force to provide prudent loan investments in a rapidly changing economy. In addition, bank lenders have the burden of federal or state regulators to manage.

Second, most loan officers spend their lending careers concentrating on underwriting thousands of various business entities. They know a little about everything, but not much about anything. Because small business loan officers are usually not specialists, they will have only an outsider's limited perspective of the mechanics of the hundreds of small business industries. They will act single-mindedly to protect the interest with which they are charged - the institution which employs them.

There are many lenders who do an exemplary job of evaluating transaction proposals according to the guidelines which their institution has chosen. But many loan officers have had to deal with great ideas that went wrong and with individuals who tried to defraud them. All lenders have been subjected to exaggerations, ineptness, and imprudence on the part of borrowers they trusted. This experience evolves into a tangible degree of caution on every new transaction succeeding the bad ones.

Some lenders, particularly regional-sized banks, have a policy of not accepting risks in commercial loans to small businesses. Their policy is to accommodate opportunities in the market so long as their funds are not truly at risk. Small businesses seeking loans should accept that decision and confine their search primarily to smaller banks or non-bank lenders with a more accommodating posture toward the small business market.

When applying for a business loan, the borrower will be required to provide considerable information designed to educate the loan officer on every aspect of the business. The purpose of this requirement is to enable the lender to evaluate the business - its management, performance, products or services, and prospects for success. But, most importantly, the lender must be convinced that the borrower understands this fundamental information and is capable of using this knowledge to succeed.

The focus of preparing a loan application should be to utilize information which is currently available to the borrower as a primary function of good management. Is the business earning money? How strong is the cash flow? What are the long term trends of the financial results?

This information protects the borrower as well as the lender, and may prevent the business from borrowing into failure. It may give the borrower notice of impending problems, providing time to change strategies and alter the business course if necessary.

The lender is an enterprise in the business of renting capital. Loans are made only in situations where the likelihood of being repaid is very high. By not being an investor, the lender avoids the risks often taken by small businesses or by venture capitalists. Lenders will always require more than one exit strategy to get the loan proceeds out of the business which usually includes collateral and personal guarantees.

The protection a lender requires for a loan provides a safeguard for the borrower as well, in the form of a second opinion of the business. While lenders are seldom experts in the borrower's industry, many will have extensive general business experience which may be helpful to the borrower's situation.

How the Lender Views a Loan Application

Lenders earn the majority of their revenue from loan interest. The lender's primary job is to make and collect good loans. However, it is easy to lose money by extending loans in a haphazard way, so lenders have developed strategies to reduce the risks associated with loans.

Most lenders use a formal loan policy to define the types of loans and the method of administering them. These policies may be made based on the particular expertise the lender employs or on the prevalent industries in the lender's geographic region.

Lending money to finance oil and gas wells in West Texas requires a different expertise than lending against wheat crops in Kansas. Lenders will generally operate within the confines of their familiarity to control the risk of their portfolio.

In a loan application the lender is seeking information. This information may be as trivial as the borrower's federal tax identification number or as detailed as projection of how fast the inventory will turnover during the next two years. All of this information helps the lender to assess the business. How well the borrower has performed in the past is a fair indicator of how well the borrower will operate in the future.

The lender has to be convinced that borrowers understand not only their products and services but also the factors that affect their businesses. The borrower must know not only the science of flipping hamburgers but also how traffic count on the street affects sales.

A frequent complaint about lenders involves the time taken to evaluate a loan proposal. Although many loan officers may seem inordinately slow, a thorough analysis of a business does require time. Mistakes are generally made by not taking enough time rather than taking too much. The loan officer's job performance will be graded more severely for loan losses than for loan successes.

Loan officers may often seem disinterested in the critical time requirements of the borrower's loan request. But the urgency does not relieve the loan officer of the inherent responsibilities of underwriting. When the borrower demands an answer too soon, that answer is always going to be no.

The better prepared the borrower is with pertinent information, the faster the loan officer can address the loan request. Since the loan officer's job is not to organize the paperwork, delivering disarranged information to the lender will slow down the review or even cause the application to be rejected.

The borrower's loan request is similar to a company's effort to sell a product. In many respects the lender is investing in people and in management. The personalities between the borrower and the lender must be compatible or the relationship will not last very long.

When listening to the comments of the loan officer, the borrower needs to be patient with the lender's lack of understanding, excitement, or enthusiasm. When the loan officer offers concerns, objections, or questions, the borrower needs to respond with measured information addressing the objections raised by the lender.

Although a commercial loan is a financial transaction, it is ultimately a relationship between lender and borrower. The key is the reciprocal comfort between the people involved.

The Five Cs of Lending

Commercial lending is an art, not a science. Based on the information provided and confirmed, loan officers have a responsibility to make lending decisions which are consistent with the parameters and limitations of their institution and with the principals of prudent lending.

Stretching these principals beyond their limitations is not good business and carries enormous risks which are not worth taking. Most denied loan requests lack a key ingredient which would make the lender confident that the funds could be repaid from the operations of the business.

Lenders test each loan application against five elementary lending criteria to determine the strength of the proposed deal. There is no magic formula or defined minimum standard of these criteria for the borrower to attain. In order to consider the loan request seriously, the lender has to be comfortable with the combined, subjective strength of these criteria.

If the borrower has an acute weakness in one of these criteria then that deficiency may or may not be overcome with a stronger position in one of the other criteria. It depends on the relative strengths and weaknesses of the borrower in each of the five criteria. These five categories include capacity, capital, collateral, credit, and character.

Capacity - The lender attempts to determine if the borrower has the "capacity" to borrow the sum requested. Are borrowers operating within the confines of their

12

abilities or are borrowers attempting to accomplish something beyond their limitations. Do the borrower's position in the market, experience in the industry, and track record in the business make the lender confident that the loan proceeds will be capably used to produce the projected results?

The lender will carefully consider whether the borrower demonstrates the effort, resolve, ingenuity, and perseverance to manage and coordinate the responsibilities necessary to generate profitable revenues and repay the loan. But if the borrower has previously obtained and repaid a loan of only $20,000, that accomplishment alone does not automatically justify the borrower's capacity for a subsequent loan of $200,000,000.

Sometimes borrowers fail to pass this test when they are more ambitious than talented. The lender must draw conclusions from the limited information provided within the application and from a few meetings with the borrower. A borrower's resume, past accomplishments, references, and capability to communicate a business strategy can contribute significantly to establishing the capacity to obtain the proposed loan.

Capital - When lenders are asked to be involved in a transaction, they attempt to quantify the adequacy of the borrower's investment. The lender will always require the borrower to have a meaningful amount of capital at risk, thereby insuring the owner's commitment to the business and reducing the lender's exposure to loss.

Capital is usually quantified as a percentage of the total business cost which must be contributed by the borrower. Different lenders have different requirements in different situations. There are varying degrees of capitalization in which a lender may favorably view the borrower's position, depending on the use of proceeds, the availability and value of collateral, and the nature of the business operation.

As the company's profits grow, the lender will watch its equity or net worth position. Lenders expect that the company's owners will permit earnings to be retained accordingly, rather than to constantly draw down all profits with dividends and distributions. While this equity-building process may cause the business owner to pay more taxes and reduce personal income, it is a reasonable expectation. The business should provide a measure of its own financing to manage a growing revenue base. This strategy makes good long-term sense for the business.

Though generally unpopular with small businesses, this requirement is significant since growth will present a new set of financial demands on the company. As sales grow, businesses invariably need new locations, new equipment, or additional working capital to absorb the increase of receivables and inventory. Allowing some of the profits to remain in the business provides for part of this needed capital and reduces future borrowing requirements.

Collateral - This criteria quantifies the borrower's ability to support the loan request with tangible assets that will guaranty repayment of the loan. Lenders prefer that the loan be supported by assets valued on a discounted basis. This discounted value provides the lender with a safe margin to cover the time and costs of converting depreciated collateral into cash should that ever be necessary.

Typically, lenders will secure the loan with a minimum of the assets being financed. But often the lender is requested to finance a sum larger than the discounted value of the financed assets. Sometimes the loan is for even more than the actual cost of the financed assets because the ancillary costs involved with their acquisition are included. Sometimes the borrower is purchasing an asset which the lender could not readily liquidate if necessary.

In these circumstances, the lender will usually require the borrower to pledge other collateral assets. This precaution insures that the lender has a comfortable margin of collateral from which to recover the loan and to be repaid if the operations of the business do not provide sufficient funds. The lender will value the collateral assets so as to maintain an adequate margin for covering the loan balance at any point in the borrower's repayment schedule, based on the rate by which the loan principal is reduced and the asset is normally depreciated. Most lenders require the borrower to produce a minimum of 100% collateral coverage on term loans.

Credit - The lender needs to evaluate the borrower's previous experience as a borrower. Studying the borrower's credit report will disclose whether the business owners have paid their previous loans as agreed. The credit report will also disclose whether the business or individuals have had civil judgments against them, unpaid tax liabilities, liens against their assets, or protection under bankruptcy court.

While clearly not an exclusive indicator of how the business will perform in the future, this information relates to how the borrower has performed in the past. Negative information in this category may give the lender an impression that the

14

borrower has not successfully overcome earlier difficulties. Poor performance with previous lenders could indicate that the borrower does not take the responsibility of repayment seriously.

Character - This criteria may be the most important assessment the loan officer can make about the loan applicant. Regardless of the positive attributes of the borrower's capacity, capital, collateral, and credit, if the borrower does not demonstrate integrity, most lenders will avoid the proposed transaction.

This criteria is probably the most subjective. Not only is it hard to define but it is also difficult to assess. There is not a checklist available to guide the loan officer's sensitivity to quantifying someone's good character.

The loan officer has to observe and study the borrower to evaluate the personal qualities of the applicant. The loan officer must watch for potential character flaws which may be detected in the attitude, conversation, perspective, or opinion of the borrower.

The borrower's character is important because it reveals intent. If the loan officer senses that the borrower has an ambivalent attitude toward fulfilling responsibilities under the proposed business deal, there is a character problem. The loan officer wants to feel that the borrower accepts a moral obligation to repay the loan even superseding the legal agreement to do so.

When a loan officer does not feel comfortable with the character of a borrower, this information will not be directly communicated to the borrower. The loan request will be denied for a different reason because the loan officer would have difficulty defending a subjective decision with definitive terms. This ambiguity is part of the intangible matrix of underwriting commercial loans.

In this age of multi-culturalism it is sometimes difficult for persons of different origins to communicate effectively. This situation can lead to misinterpretations of words and actions making it hard for one ethnic group to be comfortable with another. These culture differences certainly permeate the lending environment. The borrower and loan officer must be sensitive to such differences and invest extra time developing a business relationship to establish comfort and confidence in each other.

How Loans Are Approved

As financial institutions grow from hometown neighbors into national conglomerates the ability of an individual to single-handedly approve a commercial loan has all but vanished. Loan authority - the internal lending limits a financial institution assigns to an individual to make loans - has virtually disappeared, except when used in combination with other loan officers. Usually larger lenders provide little or no lending authority to the loan officers who interface directly with the borrowers.

Most loan officers manage customer requests and originate loans for the lender. When an attractive loan request is submitted the loan officer compiles the borrower's information, evaluates it for eligibility, and performs a measure of due diligence to confirm this information. After the loan officer concludes that the borrower's request has merit and is consistent with the lender's loan criteria, the deal is passed on for formal consideration by someone with authority to make an actual credit decision.

Depending on the size of the organization and the size of the loan request, sufficient credit authority to make a decision may go through as many as five layers of credit review to render a final answer. The two primary structures used by most lenders to make credit decisions are either the loan committee or a designated credit officer.

A credit officer is an individual in whom substantial credit authority has been vested. There may be many levels of credit officers through which transactions must be approved depending on the amount of money involved. Credit officers typically remain insulated from borrowers and depend entirely on information presented by the loan officer in deciding whether to approve a loan request.

Loan committees are usually an organized group which meets regularly to consider various loan proposals offered by its committee members or the loan officers. The size of the lending institution usually determines the size and composition of this group. In small to medium sized banks this committee will be composed of the lending officers, the chief credit officer, and the president of the institution. Most banks in this category will also seat several outside directors on their loan committees.

The loan committee hears all proposals and discusses each one according to its merits. The person sponsoring the loan application usually presents the loan request and defends it against any questions or critique from the committee. Although the presenter should be supportive of the transaction, this commitment has its limitations. The process can become somewhat political. Failure to support loan proposals introduced by other committee members can cost reciprocal support for their own loan proposals. This system obviously can be flawed with personalities and the dynamics of corporate hierarchy.

The individual sponsoring the loan request will be more successful by understanding the business and relating to the needs of the proposed borrower. The loan officer must be able to articulate these factors to the credit officer or loan committee. Too often the lack of effective communication of a proposal can slow down or eliminate viable loan opportunities in these loan approval rituals. This weakness in the process is bad for the borrower and bad for the lender.

Lenders rarely get fired for being too conservative and it is always easy to find a reason not to make a loan. Sometimes people who hold credit authority actually compete with their peers to see who can be the most conservative lender. The institution then pays a heavy price - sluggish growth and substandard income.

Through the institutional structures of credit officer and loan committee the loan request is considered by parties who are not personally involved. This process has advantages as well as disadvantages.

On the positive side, the lender is able to consider the proposed loan on a purely factual basis without the bright lights, soothing sounds, and warm feelings often evoked by the borrower to convince the lender to consider the loan. The lender can make a better financial decision operating in an emotive vacuum. The borrower can be confident that an affirmative reply reflects of the lender's recognition of a solid financial investment and commitment to a business relationship.

On the negative side, a laboratory approach to the borrower's loan request makes it difficult for the lender to consider legitimate contributing factors. Such factors can often compensate for a less than solid financial position when the lender is considering only the numbers. Businesses may fail to earn money for a variety of reasons; without taking those reasons into account, lenders sometimes miss opportunities to invest in good loan transactions.

Emerging companies may not have sterling financial histories, but may have a bright future based on market factors, new products, or premier locations not accounted for on the balance sheet of the business.

Getting SBA Approval

After the lender approves the loan request, it still must be approved by the SBA in order for the loan guaranty to be effective. The status of the lender with the SBA determines the method under which loan guaranty requests are approved. There are three distinct lender classifications utilized by the SBA:

Preferred Lender Program (PLP) - This program is a special designation by which the SBA delegates the entire guaranty approval process to the lender. The lender simply notifies the agency of any loan approvals granted under the program. Utilizing this program, the lender is usually capable of reducing the processing time required to assign an SBA loan number to the transaction to one day.

Lenders qualify for PLP status by having an exceptional performance record of loan volume and low default rates. These attributes may suggest that PLP lenders are more conservative than other participating lenders.

Certified Lender Program (CLP) - This program is a special designation by which the SBA agrees to provide accelerated processing of the lender's 7(a) loan guaranty requests. The lender agrees to provide the agency with a more thorough guaranty application and to assume additional servicing and liquidation responsibilities.

Lenders also qualify for CLP status by having a consistent performance record of loan volume and low default rates. Utilizing a CLP lender insures the borrower of faster processing by the SBA, but may also suggest that the borrower is dealing with a somewhat more conservative lender.

General Program Lender (GP) - All chartered banks and licensed SBLCs are eligible to participate in the SBA loan guaranty programs. Lenders are required to execute a standard agreement setting forth their covenant to comply with the program regulations of the SBA.

Most lenders participate under this section of the program which involves submitting loan guaranty requests on a first-come, first-served basis. Applications not completed according to agency requirements are screened out and returned to the lender for necessary modifications.

The SBA evaluates the transaction based solely on the merits demonstrated in the documentation prepared and submitted by the lender. SBA personnel usually make no visits to the business and conduct no interviews with the borrowers. As intermediary between the SBA and the borrower, the lender serves to relay questions and answers.

While each SBA district office is somewhat different, all offices are generally reasonable in their loan approval. Except for lenders with a poor track record with the SBA, the agency usually assumes that the lender has the capacity to make prudent credit decisions. However, the SBA will check the lender's credit decision for reasonableness and accuracy.

In addition, the SBA will determine that the borrower is eligible under the SBA regulations and that the proposed transaction is an acceptable use of proceeds as defined by the standard operating procedures (SOPs).

Approval of the loan proposal by the lender does not guarantee automatic SBA approval for the borrower. But if the lender is well acquainted with the SBA program and if the lender does not make any substantive errors in qualifying the proposal, the borrower can assume that SBA approval is probable.

What is the Business of the Borrower?

One of the fundamental determinants of the lender's approach to the business loan request is evaluating the industry in which the business operates. There are many inherent differences in various business categories which affect the loan risks of the lender. Many lenders will actually decide not to entertain loan requests from specific industries if they perceive the risks are beyond the comfort level within which they operate.

Before asking for consideration of financing, small business borrowers should understand they will be viewed within the industry from the lender's perspective. For instance, small business lenders feel more confident financing convenience stores which sell gasoline than financing oil and gas exploration. The risks are obviously and dramatically different at each end of this industry.

Knowing where the business stands in the vertical or horizontal scale of its industry can help the borrower prepare to meet the lender's qualifications. Understanding this information allows the borrower to position the business in a way which would yield the greatest perceptual advantage. Usually the business should project a broad view of its position. For example, instead of limiting the description of a business to flipping hamburgers, elevate that perception to help the loan officer realize that the borrower is part of the food services industry.

This heightened perspective effectively communicates the maneuverability of the business to change its business strategy according to the macro and micro economies. Realistically, the borrower can adjust its product line to follow current trends by serving grilled chicken instead of hamburgers.

Knowing how loan officers perceive and evaluate the borrower's industry and business can assist in planning the approach necessary to obtain credit. Where is the business within the life cycle of its industry? How will the business exploit its position and opportunity? This preparation will help the borrower define the risks which the lender will have to address. Then the borrower can develop a strategy to reduce those risks for the lender. If the borrower incorporates these concepts into the loan application, the loan will be easier to approve.

Lenders will evaluate the borrower's industry to determine its life cycle, estimating whether the business is beyond its financial peak (such as manufacturing buggy whips) or whether the business is too new to be an acceptable risk (such as manufacturing battery-operated automobiles). Lenders prudently require a wide public acceptance of the business products or services and prefer to finance a business before its marketing peak has occurred.

Lenders will also be wary of the borrower if the business attempts to serve too many specialized markets from a limited operating base. For example, a dry cleaner/car wash/convenience store/cappuccino bar with live music represents a unique business plan probably destined to fail. Such an operation would not have adequate focus thereby disabling effective marketing. A business should be defined in specific terms so that the loan officer clearly understands what the borrower is trying to accomplish.

How is the Business Organized?

Business entities may be organized in one of three different legal forms which determines how a lender approaches a loan request. Each business form has distinct legal characteristics and is taxed differently by the IRS. Selecting the appropriate form of business is an important decision for the borrower and should be made when the company is begun, preferably with the advice of an attorney and an accountant.

Each business form is eligible for financing assistance from the SBA.

Proprietorship - This form of business organization is for individuals who have chosen to sell products or provide services without the creation of a separate legal entity. The business is embodied in the efforts of the individual, who may use a distinctive business name or title. The business name does not carry protection from duplication and the individual carries full legal and financial liability for all acts of the enterprise. A proprietor's income is taxed as business income on Schedule C of the IRS form 1040.

Partnership - This form of business organization is for two or more individuals who choose to formalize their business relationship in a registered partnership. Partnerships may be defined as general or limited, each of which provides distinct definitions of the responsibilities of the individual partners.

In brief, general partnerships divide the responsibility of their activities equally among the partners on a prorated basis of ownership. Limited partnerships may limit the responsibility and liability of the limited partners for the activities of the partnership. Limited partnerships have a general partner who accepts the liability for the actions of the partnership.

Partnerships are usually taxed by prorating any gains or losses among the partners, as provided for in the partnership agreement.

Corporation - This form of business organization is a distinct business entity organized by one or more individual "shareholders" who have certain rights under the protection of the corporate entity. Generally, shareholders are not exposed to any of the liabilities of the corporation unless they purposely elect to guaranty specific liabilities of the corporation.

The two primary forms of corporations are the "C - corporation" and the "S - corporation." Although similar, these forms differ in that an S - corporation is intended to provide smaller companies the advantage of lower tax liability by passing profits or losses through to the shareholders on a pro rata basis similar to a partnership. In contrast, C - corporation earnings are taxable and the shareholders are also taxed on any distributions or dividends paid out by the corporation. And distributions by C - corporations are not deductible from the corporations' taxable income thereby causing the distributed monies to be taxed twice.

In recent years many states have created an entity known as a "Limited Liability Corporation" (LLC), which offers many of the favorable liability protections of a corporation and the favorable taxation attributes of a partnership.

Why Borrow Money?

Borrowed money is expensive and represents an additional business risk for the company seeking to obtain it. In conjunction with the normal business risks associated with building new facilities or launching new products, borrowing money involves a compound layer of management. The borrower's new partner (the lender) may not be as patient as is sometimes needed, particularly if things do not go as planned. The lender may have higher expectations for the financial results than the market can deliver in a given time frame.

Careful consideration is recommended for any business seeking to borrow funds because of the potential risk of not succeeding. Rather than maximizing the available leverage, businesses should understand the advantages of mineralizing the portion of borrowed monies in order to reduce the company's exposure.

Defining the exact reason a business requires a loan is the first step toward the application process. Qualified borrowers lose precious time and credibility by not establishing a succinct financing scheme to determine how much capital is needed and how it will be used. An unfocused borrower makes lenders nervous. It is difficult to feel confident about a business which wants to acquire a large imprecise loan to sink into an enterprise without defining how it will be absorbed and what results are intended.

Business owners must be able to specify exactly why they need financing and exactly what impact it will have. Failure to articulate this information reflects

22

either unprepared or inadequate management, or the existence of another agenda in which the lender should not participate.

Time is frequently wasted by small business owners seeking to borrow money from the wrong lender through their failure to define the kind of money they need. Too many institutions reject these inappropriate applications without referring borrowers to the correct lender.

Understanding that certain lenders service specific types of loans can make the search for financing much easier and more successful. There are four major reasons for a business to borrow money. Each of these reasons requires distinctive underwriting and repayment terms:

Real Estate Loans - Whether for acquisition, construction, or improvement, real estate loans seem to be the most popular loans for most small business lenders. These are typically long-term loans which on the average have the safest collateral available to lenders. The best terms offered on SBA loans for commercial real estate usually include a 25 year amortization of principal and interest. Interest rates on loans of this term are normally floating so the lender can avoid extended exposure to under-market rates.

Start-Up Loans - Start-up financing is needed by some borrowers to supplement their own equity contributions when purchasing a business operation or when launching a business. Most lenders require the borrower to have strong collateral or other compensating factors to justify the risks involved with this kind of financing. Start-up money is hard to obtain if the borrower cannot supply a sizable contribution of personal capital, usually a minimum of 25-30% of the total financing needed. Being the most difficult financing to obtain, start-up loans can test the new business owner's resolve to begin the business.

Equipment Loans - Equipment loans are intermediate-term loans that provide funds to purchase equipment assets. They are usually repaid over a term of no more than the expected useful life of the equipment assets financed. The best terms offered on SBA loans for equipment usually include a 10 year amortization of principal and interest. Interest rates on loans of this term are normally floating so the lender can avoid extended exposure to under-market rates.

Working Capital Loans - This financing is provided to assist the business with operating cash to produce profitable revenues. If the borrower can offer capital assets as collateral, these loans are sometimes offered over a long term on a limited basis. This kind of loan is essentially a substitute for capital.

Working capital financing often involves advancing loans against the accounts receivable and inventory assets of a business on a short-term, revolving basis. That is, the loan balance moves frequently with draws and repayments from the borrower on a negotiated basis, depending on the accounts receivable and inventory balances of the business.

When current assets are used to secure this financing, they must be constantly monitored to assure the lender of adequate collateral coverage and to provide the lender with an updated, reliable value of these assets. This supervision is expensive and is paid for by the borrower which significantly increases the costs of the financing.

Adjusting the Borrower's Attitude

Borrowers are better prepared when they recognize the dynamics of the loan application process. Approaching the process with a realistic attitude enhances the borrower's loan application and increases the chances of success.

Here is the lender's "Golden Rule:" *those with the gold make the rules.* During the application process the borrower provides an enormous volume of information, answers many arcane questions, and is scrutinized over trivial details of the business. This repetitive and tedious process is not personal in intent; it is a business procedure.

The borrower is asking for a service that requires subjective qualification and objective quantification. One business (the borrower) is asking another business (the lender) for an investment of time and funds. The application process, by necessity, is laborious but meaningful. Most lenders see many hundreds of loan requests every year.

A borrower should plan ahead and initiate the loan request before it is needed. By rushing the process, the borrower dampens the lender's enthusiasm about the loan request and creates suspicions that facts are being distorted or concealed. Even if the borrower is approved for a loan, missteps in the application or approval process can weaken the relationship with the lender from the beginning, which can haunt the borrower later.

Information is a powerful tool for supporting the business loan application. The borrower's understanding of the industry, the competition, the market, and even the economy can support the representations the borrower may be depending on to boost the loan request. This pertinent data will make the lender more confident about the borrower's capability to repay the loan.

The front-line personnel with whom the borrower directly interfaces may not present an impressive business acumen and often they will not have had as much business experience as the borrower. But the lender has selected this person to perform an important screening process for eliminating the numerous proposals that are undefined or unrealistic.

Although appreciating the difficulty of the lender's role does not insure approval of the proposed loan, the borrower will benefit by understanding the requirements of the lender's job. Cooperation and patience throughout this process are necessary for successfully obtaining a loan.

Researching the Lending Market

Too many small business owners watch television. The best source of information to find small business financing is definitely not creative television advertising, clever radio ads, glossy magazine ads.

A practical rule is that the lenders with the fanciest advertising are the most difficult lenders from which to get a loan. Why do the largest banks spend so much money on an advertising when they already have a high public profile and their branches seem to be everywhere?

One reason is that, in comparison to their smaller competitors, these larger banks have more stringent credit standards and they turn down a higher percentage of loan applications. Therefore, these lenders need a larger stream of applications in order to find the loan requests they will approve.

How should a borrower find a lender which is interested in small businesses? Borrowers need to research the market for lenders that address the small business sector. The best place to begin this research is at the SBA District Office in the district in which the borrower is located.

The SBA can provide information about local lenders that participate in the SBA loan guaranty program. The SBA can also disclose the total dollar amount of loans made by any specific lender in that district in preceding periods. Evaluating this information along with other public information will reveal if SBA lending is important to a prospective lender.

For example, all federally and state regulated banks are required to make copies of their financial statement available to the public. Comparing the total commercial loan volume to the total SBA loan volume will be indicative of how significant SBA lending is to the bank's commercial loan portfolio.

Another important factor is the size of the bank relative to the size of its SBA portfolio. If a $2 billion dollar bank can deliver only $10 million in SBA loans, and a $70 million bank can make $15 million in SBA loans, it is obvious which lender has the stronger interest in the small business market.

A borrower should interview the commercial loan officers from several local lenders to determine if they make small business loans. Prior to applying for a loan the borrower needs to determine if the lender would seriously consider the specific kind of transaction the borrower is seeking. Which lender would be likely to consider the loan proposal?

The borrower should be aware that some banks are not in optimum financial condition. For a variety of reasons some banks perform inadequately and even fail. Poor management, bad investments, and unsound business practices are problems encountered by banks as well as other businesses.

Bank financial problems do not occur suddenly. Since regulated either by federal or state banking supervisors, a bank's performance is a matter of public record. There are many sources of information about a particular bank to which the borrower may refer. One source is Bauer Financial Reports, Inc. which monitors the performance of banks and rates them according to their financial condition and performance. These reports are available to anyone needing to access prospective bank lenders and may be obtained by calling Bauer at 800-388-6686.

Other sources of information on potential lenders may be the borrower's CPA, other business owners, or even business competitors. Virtually every small business needs financing at some time. Establishing a prospective list of lenders early in the process is well worth the effort.

Getting A Second Opinion

It is wise to test the loan application on the borrower's closest advisors before taking it to a lender for review. Sometimes in the rush to complete the voluminous set of documents, the preparer can lose sight of errors in providing support information or omissions in detailing plans and projections. Having other parties review this data before it is submitted to the lender can reduce the chances of mistakes and hopefully eliminate an embarrassing presentation.

Employees from the appropriate departments should review specific sections of the information to proof the work for errors or omissions. For example, the marketing department can review the presentation of the company's marketing plan, while the operations department can review a description of the company's production details. This exercise will separate the preparer from the documentation for a few days, improving the preparer's focus, and insuring the inclusion of important details.

After each section has been reviewed by the various departments of the company, the financial or accounting personnel should review the entire set of data for completeness and accuracy. These employees will have a high degree of familiarity with the entire business operation and will be capable of reviewing the big picture.

If a business does not have people in positions capable of providing this review, the application information can be reviewed by the company's CPA, business advisor, or a loan consultant. The proposal should always be given a second opinion before it leaves the borrower's office.

Giving the Application a Trial Run

In its formation stages an application can be tested in a preliminary interview with a lender. This exploratory meeting is not intended to establish a banking relationship between the borrower and lender; rather it is used to define general parameters of the proposed loan.

In these discussions the borrower should talk (not write) about the proposed loan regarding its size, term, use of proceeds, and collateral. The lender in response will indicate the feasibility and limitations of the loan transaction.

Since this preliminary discussion is designed to assist with preparation of a final proposal, the borrower need not select the most appropriate lender. Nor should the borrower leave any written information in the lender's files which may affect how the bank would structure the proposed loan or which could be compared to an amended application.

If there are any special circumstances which would need to be explained or which would require additional attention, this information should be saved for the end of the discussion. The focus of the conversation should be on the positive: how would the lender approach the deal and what can be done. Once the potential for a deal is determined, other conditions can be introduced to determine how the lender can work with or around them.

Because this exercise is intended to be a trial run to access the lending community, the borrower can avoid commitment to a particular loan request until learning how the lender reacts. The borrower thereby gains insight and information about changes which would strengthen the approach and plans.

Sometimes, understandably, loan officers refuse to be specific about transactions until borrowers provide more information in writing. This reaction need not eliminate a lender from the prospect list, but rather prompts the borrower to interview a different lender from whom information might be obtained.

Timing Is Important

To maximize the impact of the borrower's presentation of a loan proposal, smart scheduling is important and is based on calculated criteria. Serious borrowers make an appointment to see the lender rather than arriving unexpectedly. Without discussing the proposal over the phone, the borrower should tell the loan officer the purpose of the appointment and how much time is needed to present the loan request. A prepared borrower needs a minimum of an hour of the loan officer's full attention without interruption. Timing the presentation is essential to maximizing its impact and increasing the borrower's chances of approval.

Most loan officers appreciate this planning in order to reserve sufficient time to focus on what the borrower wants to discuss. Requesting an appointment will communicate that the borrower is serious about the presentation and that the loan officer's undivided attention is expected.

When making an appointment with a loan officer, some meeting times can be better than other times. For example, if the lender is a bank, the first and fifteenth days of the month may be disadvantageous if the lender is also responsible for approving bank teller transactions. Those two days are the busiest days of the month for payroll deposits, government check cashing, and benefit payment receipt. The lender could be constantly interrupted with frivolous questions and check approvals.

Mondays and Fridays should also be avoided. Loan officers are often subjected to more demands on these days, due to the natural interruption of work flow caused by the weekend. They seem to have more continuous control of their time Tuesday through Thursday. Within this time frame, morning meeting are more favorable that afternoons.

Although many people are impressed when treated to lunch by a banker, the invitation does not indicate any elevation of the borrower's desirability to the lender. In addition, lunch meetings are usually too congested with the distractions of movement, people, and food to get the full attention the borrower needs for the loan proposal. Trying to share any written information in that scenario is frustrating. At this stage, the borrower needs the privacy and seclusion of an office.

It is possible to determine - and avoid - time periods when lenders are being audited by regulators. During the audit, which usually lasts from two to three weeks, the lender is often deluged with requests for information from the auditors, which could make this period a difficult one to get the attention the borrower needs.

Of course, the primary determinant of when the applicant can meet with the loan officer is when the borrower's business permits. Important duties at the business are the primary and controlling priorities.

Projecting the Revenues, Expenses, and Income

Financing is based on a simple principle: lenders always require the borrower to agree that the loan will be repaid. At the time the loan request is submitted, the lender will evaluate the borrower's ability to repay the loan with funds generated by the business. This analysis is extremely important and is integral to the borrower's ability to get a loan.

The bank will expect the borrower to provide realistic projections about how the invested proceeds of the loan will generate revenues for the borrower. Further, the borrower should identify additional costs which are necessary to produce these revenues, and calculate the resulting profits from which the borrower will repay the loan.

The integrity and reasonableness of these projections are often the single most important factor in granting loan approval. In constructing these financial projections, management must be honest not only with the lender, but also with themselves; representing unrealistic figures is not only unethical, but also self-defeating.

The lender is usually not an expert in the borrower's field and may not recognize aggressive revenue projections. Failure to exercise prudence and good judgment can place the company - and the borrower's own financial stability - at risk if money is borrowed which cannot be paid back as scheduled.

Financial projections take into account the estimated operating results of the business for a defined period in the future. Most lenders require seeing these operating results projected for a minimum of two years. It is useful to project the first twelve months on a month-to-month basis, in order to demonstrate the immediate effects of the borrowed money on the current business cash cycle. Projecting financial results beyond twenty-fours months is difficult due to multiple factors and economic cycles which may not be anticipated or easily predicted.

In developing the operating projections, the borrower should use a model which resembles the business profit/loss statement (sometimes referred to as a pro forma) and insert the estimated figures accordingly. The starting date should coincide with the date the borrower would reasonably expect the loan to be funded. The projections should be aligned with the beginning of the company's next fiscal year.

Written details are necessary to explain and substantiate estimates of significant entries, such as revenues and major costs. And rather than being over overloaded with rows of meaningless trivia, the projection model should be streamlined by combining the many itemized accounts into primary revenue and expense categories.

For example, the many different expenses of hiring, compensating, motivating, providing benefits to, and paying taxes for employees should be projected as "Salaries" rather than detailed into several line items. This larger, general category would include all related expenses, such as actual salaries, payroll taxes, unemployment insurance premiums, employee benefits, employee insurance costs, payroll processing costs, and other direct expenses attributable to the payroll of the business.

Specific accounts of the "Salaries" expense category can be detailed in the footnotes, readily found if requested but not distracting from the main text. This exercise helps the borrower organize information better and keeps the lender focused on the big picture of the financial projections.

Providing the loan officer with line-by-line calculations of the expected revenues or expenses would create hundreds of additional and extraneous questions. The borrower does not want the loan officer to micro-manage the business nor to lose sight of the overall projected results.

Producing this projection model will assist the borrower's planning and subject the proposal to a financial litmus test. The most important guideline is to be realistic. The borrower needs to demonstrate confidence in the projected revenues and particularly in the real costs of producing those revenues.

A commonly used profit/loss projection model is shown on Illustration 2-A. It is easy to modify this model to match the borrower's financial reporting, simply by changing the revenue or expense entries to correspond to the borrower's financial statement. The borrower's projection model should usually include the following primary categories:

Income:

Sales / Revenues -   Monies expected to be received by the business in payment for services provided or products sold to its customers.

Cost of Goods Sold -   Expenses which represent a direct cost associated with producing or acquiring the products sold by the business. (If the borrower is not sure about exactly which expenses to include here, the company's CPA should be consulted.)

| *Gross Profit -* | The result of subtracting the Costs of Goods Sold from the Total Sales / Revenues. |

Expenses:

| *Salaries -* | Labor costs (except for labor costs included in the Cost of Goods Sold), the company's FICA tax contributions, unemployment taxes, benefit insurance, and other direct costs incurred by the business to acquire labor. |

| *Management Salaries -* | Optional entry to define the labor expense of the company's management. Lenders are often interested in how well the borrower plans to reward management and owners. |

| *Administrative -* | Costs associated with managing the operation, such as office supplies, petty cash, refreshments, light equipment maintenance, copier supplies, and other small expenses associated with the administrative functions of the borrower. |

| *Advertising -* | Expenses for marketing and advertising the business such as brochures, newspaper ads, radio spots, television commercials, yellow page ads, corporate gifts, direct mail, telemarketing, and other efforts to promote sales. |

| *Bank Fees -* | Costs of banking fees (except interest on loans). Typically a business which might incur large bank fees is one which issues a large number of checks, requires a significant volume of cash inventory, makes frequent deposits, or utilizes a merchant account for credit card processing. This category should be used only if the estimated expenses are expected to exceed about five percent of the company's total projected expenses. If the bank fees are not a significant part of the expenses, they should be included in the Administrative Expenses. |

32

Illustration 2-A

Profit / Loss Projections

Business Name:_____

	Interim period ending	Proforma Year 1	Proforma Year 2
TOTAL REVENUES	$_____	$_____	$_____
COST OF GOODS	_____	_____	_____
GROSS PROFIT	$_____	$_____	$_____

EXPENSES:

Officer's Salaries	_____	_____	_____
Salaries & Payroll Taxes	_____	_____	_____
Other Payroll Expenses	_____	_____	_____
Repairs/Maintenance	_____	_____	_____
Bad Debts	_____	_____	_____
Rents	_____	_____	_____
Taxes & Licenses	_____	_____	_____
Depreciation & Amortization	_____	_____	_____
Advertising & Marketing	_____	_____	_____
Employee Benefits	_____	_____	_____
Telephone	_____	_____	_____
Utilities	_____	_____	_____
Accounting & Legal Expenses	_____	_____	_____
Insurance	_____	_____	_____
Miscellaneous	_____	_____	_____
Total Expenses	_____	_____	_____
TOTAL OPERATING PROFIT	$_____	$_____	$_____
Interest-SBA loan	_____	_____	_____
Interest- All Other	_____	_____	_____
Total Interest Expense	_____	_____	_____
NET INCOME	$_____	$_____	$_____

Depreciation/Amortization - Non-cash expenses based on the useful life of capital assets or the acceptable amortization period recommended by the CPA. These expenses affect the profitability of the business, but not the cash flow. Use of these expenses will help the borrower estimate the taxable income of the business. These entries are added back to the company's net income when projecting the operation's cash flow.

Entertainment/Travel - Direct costs of entertaining prospective clients, traveling on sales calls or to trade conferences, or other general purposes not attributable to the direct production of income. This category should be used if the estimated expenses are expected to exceed five percent of the company's total projected expenses. If the entertainment or travel are not a large part of the expenses, they should be included in Administrative or Advertising categories.

Equipment - Annual expenses for light equipment assets which are acquired with the entire expense recognized in the same year, or equipment which is leased. Equipment maintenance and repair expenses should be included in this paragraph. This category should also be used only if the estimated expenses are expected to exceed about five percent of the company's total projected expenses. If equipment costs are not a significant part of the expenses, they should be included in the Administrative or Miscellaneous Expenses.

Insurance - Expenses for general liability insurance, workers compensation insurance, and other insurance products purchased by the business (except employee benefit insurance). This category should be used only if the estimated expenses are expected to exceed about five percent of the company's total projected expenses. If insurance expenses are not a significant part of the expenses, they should be included in the Administrative Expenses.

Postage/Courier - Costs of postage, postage equipment, courier fees, and special handling costs (such as certified mail). This category should be used if the relative expense is a notable percentage of the operating cost. If the postage or courier expenses are not a significant part of total expenses, these expenses should be included in the Administrative Expense.

Professional Fees - Expenses for any professional services anticipated for the business (such as legal, accounting, or tax) including the expenses associated with obtaining and closing the proposed SBA financing.

Rent/Occupancy - Costs of occupancy, CAM charges, and other expenses associated with the business premises (such as utilities, repairs, and real estate taxes).

Telephone - Costs of the basic telephone service, long distance, answering services, communication equipment rental, and other expenses related to providing telephone communication for the business.

Miscellaneous - Various costs which are not defined in the other categories, but which must be recognized. This entry should be relatively small. If it exceeds ten percent of the expenses projected, then additional categories should be introduced for any group of costs which total comparably with the other other categories used in the projections.

Total Operating Expenses - Total the sum of projected Expense categories.

Operating Profit - Gross Profit minus Total Expenses (also referred to as EBIT - Earnings Before Interest and Taxes).

Interest -	Interest expenses expected to be charged for the loan balances during the period. It is important to use the actual interest rate and loan amortization period for all existing liabilities and to calculate the proposed financing according to the terms requested.
Income Taxes [1] -	Federal and state income taxes, based on any profits projected.
Net Profit -	Operating Profit minus Interest and Income Taxes

[1] - Most lenders are interested in the borrower's projected operating profit, and may not notice nor be concerned if income tax liabilities are not estimated. Because of the calculation complexities involved, tax credits or loss carryforwards which may be available, and changing tax rates, an estimation of these costs can be very time-consuming for a relatively inaccurate result.

Projecting Cash Flow

The income projection will provide the borrower with the expected profits (or losses) of the business. The next stage is to develop a cash flow projection. How do the operating results relate to the balance sheet? What cash will be available to cover operating expenditures and to service debt?

In a basic cash flow model, the non-cash expenses (depreciation and amortization) and interest expenses are added to the company's net profit. This calculation provides a quick summary of the total cash available to service the projected debt.

- *Cash Available for Debt Service* - This figure is derived as follows:

    Net Profit + Depreciation & Amortization + Interest Expenses

From this cash balance is subtracted the company's total principal and interest payments for the projection period, including the existing debt and the debt service of the proposed debt. The resulting number is the net cash flow from operations.

- *Net Cash Flow* - This figure is derived as follows:

Cash Available for Debt Service - Total Principal & Interest Payments

From this analysis, the lender will be primarily interested in learning the ratio of the borrower's cash flow to the total debt payments required to service the proposed loan.

- *Debt Service Coverage Ratio* - This ratio is calculated as follows:

$$\frac{\text{Cash Available for Debt Service}}{\text{Total Principal \& Interest Payments}}$$

This ratio measures the company's ability to meet its scheduled obligations and to service its debt. By comparing cash available to the required debt payments, this ratio indicates how well a business is managing its existing debt and its capacity to take on new loans. If this ratio is less than 1x, then the company is not projected to have sufficient cash to meet its existing or projected payments.

Most lenders require this ratio to be 1.2x, or higher, depending on their loan policy and the borrower's situation. If the cash flow projections do not result in an adequate Debt Service Coverage Ratio, it is important to review all of the borrower's revenue and expense estimates. If the borrower cannot reconcile these figures according to the company's true estimates, then the loan request will probably have to be reduced to a level which can be serviced by the profits produced with a smaller loan.

A more sophisticated management tool is to utilize a month-to-month cash flow projection model, which tracks revenues and expenses in monthly increments. The elementary example discussed above does not account for accounts receivable (credit sales), trade accounts (credit purchases), and other variables which will affect the company's cash flow.

Using a month-to-month pro forma enables the borrower to account for all such variables, and to be more accurate in predicting the cash flow of the business. A detailed legend is necessary for explaining the borrower's assumptions in developing the pro forma.

Illustration 2-B

Monthly Cash Flow Projection

Prepared by: _____ Date: _____

Name of Business: _____

MONTH NUMBER MONTH NAME YEAR:	Startup Cash Position	1 Estimate	2 Estimate	3 Estimate	4 Estimate	5 Estimate	6 Estimate	7 Estimate	8 Estimate	9 Estimate	10 Estimate	11 Estimate	12 Estimate	Total Estimate
Cash On Hand														---
Cash Receipts														
Cash sales														
Credit account collections														
Loan or other cash injection														
Total Cash Receipts														
Total Cash Available														
Cash Paid Out														
Purchases														
Gross wages														
Payroll expenses														
Outside services														
Supplies														
Repairs/maintenance														
Advertising														
Car, delivery, & travel														
Accounting & legal														
Rent														
Telephone														
Utilities														
Insurance														
Taxes														
Interest-SBA loan														
Interest- All Other														
Other (specify)														
Miscellaneous														
Subtotal of expenses														
Principal repay-SBA														
Principal repay														
Total Cash Paid Out														
Cash (end of month)														

A commonly used cash flow projection model is shown on Illustration 2-B. It is easy to modify this model to match the borrower's financial reporting, simply by making changes to the revenue or expense entries to match the company's financial statement. Other variables which have an impact on the borrower's cash flow should also be demonstrated.

Other Financial Analysis

Loan officers will use a number of financial ratios in analyzing the borrower's financial position to determine the strength of the company. Various tests are used to determine the relative liquidity, leverage, coverage, and operating performance of the business in comparison to a composite of other businesses with a similar size in the borrower's industry.

Depending on the borrower's capability to produce these calculations and the depth of analysis the borrower can objectively determine, these ratios can be applied to the company's financial results to learn what should be expected from the loan officer's evaluation. Positive results will be helpful to the loan proposal by accentuating the financial strength of the business and demonstrating the acumen and the sophistication of the borrower's financial management.

Some of the more common ratios are discussed below with an explanation of how they are calculated and what information they provide. There are no right or wrong results - these figures measure the borrower's financial position in relative terms which can be compared to other businesses. Most lenders use the Robert Morris Associates (RMA) Annual Statement Studies© as a guideline for industry norms in comparatively analyzing financial ratios.

The RMA Studies gather voluntary submissions of financial statements from thousands of businesses in every industry, as defined by the Standard Industrial Code (SIC). These financial statements are compiled and averaged to determine the median and mean of operating standards for every industry each year. These results are published by each SIC category in order to provide information about the relative financial condition and performance of each industrial sector.

Liquidity Ratios:

● *Current Ratio* - This ratio is calculated as follows:

$$\frac{\text{Total Current Assets}}{\text{Total Current Liabilities}}$$

This ratio is a rough measurement of the company's ability to pay its current liabilities with its current assets. It reveals the relative strength or weakness of the working capital, which is the result of subtracting current liabilities from current assets. A higher current ratio is the result of stronger working capital, indicating the excess of current assets over current liabilities. The composition and quality of current assets are critically important to understanding the liquidity of a business.

● *Quick Ratio (Acid Test)* - This ratio is calculated as follows:

$$\frac{\text{Cash \& Equivalents \& Receivables}}{\text{Total Current Liabilities}}$$

Dubbed the "acid test," this ratio provides a more difficult test of liquidity based on existing cash assets and those assets likely to be converted to cash in the current period. A result of less than 1:1 might mean that the business is relying on the conversion of inventory or other assets to liquidate current liabilities.

● *Sales / Receivables* -This ratio is calculated as follows:

$$\frac{\text{Net Sales}}{\text{Trade Receivables (net)}}$$

This ratio measures the number of times the accounts receivable are fully collected, or "turn over" during the year. If a company's ratio equals twelve, that means that the receivables turn over twelve times a year. A higher ratio means a shorter time between sales and cash collection. If a company's ratio is smaller than the rest of its industry, then the quality of the company's receivables or the company's credit and collection policies may need to be examined.

● *Days' Receivables* - This ratio is calculated as follows:

$$\frac{365}{\text{Sales / Receivables Ratio}}$$

This ratio expresses the Sales / Receivables Ratio in the average number of days required to collect an account receivable. This ratio may be indicative of the control a company has over its credit policy and the quality of its account receivables.

- *COGS / Inventory* - This ratio is calculated as follows:

$$\frac{\text{Cost of Sales}}{\text{Inventory}}$$

This ratio measures the number of times the inventory is completely used, or "turns over" during the year. If a company's ratio equals twelve, that means that the inventory turns over twelve times a year. The higher ratio indicates that the inventory is turning more often, which usually means the company has better liquidity or good merchandising. If a company's ratio is smaller than the rest of its industry, then the company's inventory may not be selling, may be obsolete, or may be overstocked.

- *Days' Inventory* - This ratio is calculated as follows:

$$\frac{365}{\text{COGS/Inventory Ratio}}$$

This ratio expresses the COGS / Inventory Ratio in the average number of days required to use the inventory on hand. This ratio may be indicative of the quality of inventory management or the quality of the inventory.

- *Cost of Goods Sold / Payables* - This ratio is calculated as follows:

$$\frac{\text{Cost of Goods Sold}}{\text{Trade Payables}}$$

This ratio measures the number of times the company's trade payables are paid off, or "turn over" during the year. The larger this ratio, the shorter the time between the company's purchases and subsequent payment for goods. If the company's ratio is lower than the industry average, then there may be a liquidity problem causing the company to pay its bills slowly.

Leverage Ratio:

- *Debt / Worth* - This ratio is calculated as follows:

$$\frac{\text{Total Liabilities}}{\text{Net Worth}}$$

This ratio measures the size of the owner's equity capital relative to the lender's debt capital. By determining the relative investment provided by the owners, it defines the degree of risk assumed by the lenders.

Operating Ratios:

- *% Profit Before Taxes / Total Assets* - This ratio is calculated as follows:

$$\frac{\text{Profit Before Taxes}}{\text{Total Assets}}$$

$$\text{X} \quad 100$$

In measuring the pre-tax return on total assets, this ratio reflects the efficiency with which management is employing the company's assets. Lower than average ratios may suggest a problem with the company's profitability.

- *Sales / Total Assets* - This ratio is calculated as follows:

$$\frac{\text{Net Sales}}{\text{Total Assets}}$$

This ratio measures the company's ability to generate sales based on its total asset strength. It is useful in comparing the effectiveness of a company's management and sales effort relative to other companies in the industry.

A problem with many of these ratios is that they compare one day's financial position in annualized terms. Because they cannot take a company's seasonality into account, they may be skewed by circumstances which distort the results.

There are no good or bad ratios; they are always relative. Even if the borrower's particular financial performance is very impressive, the company may not compare well with the results of the RMA study because of extraordinary reasons. These studies will not guaranty that the loan proposal is approved or rejected.

But the information is useful for understanding how the company compares to other companies in the same business. Based on this data, the borrower can explain differences between the company's performance and the industry norms.

While there are additional ratios published by the RMA, the ratios included above will give the borrower a general understanding of the information the loan officer is using to evaluate the business. A more thorough explanation of the ratios and a current edition of the RMA Annual Statement Studies, can be requested through Robert Morris Associates in Philadelphia, PA at (215) 851-0585.

Chapter 3

Preparing A Loan Application

Getting Organized

When applying for business loans, people are often surprised about the extensive degree of information that the lender will require. This information provides the lender with details about such items as the borrower's loan request, status of the business, use of the loan proceeds, value of collateral assets, and financial condition of the business and business owners.

The size of the loan request will not necessarily enlarge - nor shorten - this list of requirements. The lender's responsibility to understand the borrower's situation, financial condition, and prospects for repayment is constant, whether the loan is for thousands or millions of dollars. Obviously, the degree of scrutiny will be greater on larger transactions, but the borrower's command of this information is important, regardless of the size of the loan proposal.

There is no comprehensive list of required information since every deal is different. The list of suggested information presented in this chapter is fairly complete, but may either too inclusive or perhaps exclusive of items needed for the loan application. That is because no two loans are alike - the lender, the borrower, the business, and the situation are all unique in every transaction, with very little duplication.

There are hundreds of variables which can change the specific information requirements of the lender. Even the lender will not know everything that is needed until the review process begins.

Applying for a business loan requires the borrower to educate the lender about the business and its owners with a customized set of standard documentation, much of which is prepared specifically for each particular application. These documents will disclose an enormous amount of information from which the lender will determine whether the borrower qualifies for a loan in accordance with the lender's requirements.

This chapter defines many items frequently requested by lenders, describes exactly what the lender is looking for, and discusses why this information is needed. Further, it will suggest how to anticipate questions from the loan officers and how to prepare answers in advance. Assimilation of this process will enhance and accelerate the loan request.

Most of the information, documents, and records needed by the borrower is detailed in this chapter, organized in specific categories and in the logical order for discussing these topics with the loan officer when the borrower presents the loan proposal. It is recommended that the proposal be introduced to the lender in person in order to benefit from the most effective and persuasive technique for selling the loan; the sales abilities of the borrower's management.

However, it is necessary to leave the loan officer with a written summary of the proposal to document exactly what the borrower is seeking. The loan officer can later refer back to the written information when beginning to review the specifics of the request.

The borrower's level of preparation and the borrower's degree of cooperation will communicate to the loan officer how desirable the applicant will be as a customer. If it is difficult to get the borrower to respond to the lender's request for documentation and information before the loan is closed, then the loan officer will recognize that it will be even more difficult to get such information after the loan is made. When the borrowers are responsive and cooperative in meeting these requests for information, they demonstrate management capabilities, they bolster their efforts to receive a loan, and they also facilitate consideration of the proposed loan.

Much of the data suggested in this chapter does not exist in the form of a specific document. For purposes of supplying this required information to the lender, memoranda can be designed to document the facts, figures and information in writing. Emphasis should be on completeness, conciseness, logical sequence accuracy, and clarity.

Submitting information to promote the business is undermined when there are grammatical errors, misspelled words, and incoherent ideas. With the availability of high quality word processing software, many of these errors can be eliminated. There is no excuse for poorly written information communicated incorrectly and haphazardly.

When supplying information to the lender the borrower should assume that the lender does not understand the industry jargon or abbreviations. Technical terms and methodologies should be explained to that insure the lender can follow the reasoning of the loan proposal. For example, if a loan officer doesn't understand how local health ordinances mandate certain minimum standards for food processing, then they may not recognize how the borrower can justify the expensive expenditures required to build a commercial kitchen. In assuming that the lender has no familiarity with the business, the application will need to document every nuance about what the borrower wants to do and how the borrower proposes to pay for it.

Too many small businesses pay thousands of dollars annually for the preparation of financial statements without truly understanding what this information can disclose. The bank will carefully study the balance sheet, income statement, and sources and uses of cash. By analyzing financial trends and ratios, the bank will evaluate the strength of the company and will even compare it to other companies in the industry. By determining the positive (or negative) direction of the financial results, the lender will assess the risks of lending money to the borrower. The loan officer is primarily interested in the borrower's ability to produce future funds to repay the lender.

In addition, the loan officer will check the company's credit history, appraise the collateral, check references, verify account balances, and test the financial projections of future performance in order to assess the risk associated with providing capital to the applicant.

When initiating the application process for a business loan, it is wise for the borrower to know not only the details of the documentation but also what the lender's analysis will conclude. Sometimes there are periods of lower performance or other events which will raise the concern of the lender. The borrower should prepare to discuss those exceptions and to produce documentation to support the explanation. By anticipating the need for these items, the borrower can demonstrate the relevant skills of organization and competence in financial affairs.

The lender will need information in several distinct categories. Although there is no official format, the borrower's assemblage should be organized to assist the loan officer in compiling the information easier and evaluating it quickly. This compilation method is more efficient and in better sequence than submitting information in a business plan.

Due to the typically large volume of material, it is more useful to arrange the information in a series of large, open-ended folders, rather than using ring binders, clamps, or color-coded tabs. This system permits the loan officer to access and to file each section independently. Much of the information will have to be copied for various parties to review it, and this duplication can be done more easily if the documents are not bound in any way. Most SBA loan officers will discard any binding which interferes with their access to the raw data.

It is important to provide clean, clear documents which are entirely legible. Everything should be reviewed prior to submission to eliminate incorrect compilation, incomplete pages, poor copy production, or out-of-sequence documentation. These logistic errors distract the loan officer from the business information being submitted by the borrower.

Original documents should not be submitted unless there are several copies, such as the company's financial statement. Any copied document may be authenticated, if necessary, with a dated original signature on the margin of the cover page of any document.

Finally, if the borrower cannot produce a particular document or other information requested by the loan officer, an honest explanation is important to provide a legitimate reason and a time-frame for availability. If, for example, company operations are overloaded at that moment and no one can stop to prepare the information, the borrower will be demonstrating that the business priorities are in correct order.

It is a mistake for the borrower to blame the unavailability of information on the company's accountant, attorney, bookkeeper, or any other party. If these parties cannot be managed by the borrower, who is paying them for professional assistance, how can the borrower manage other operations to repay the lender's loan?

If information is not available due to reasons which cannot be resolved immediately, then the borrower should consider delaying the initiation of the loan application. For example, if the borrower is not able to obtain the most recent financial statements because the accountant has not been paid for last year's financial statement, then the borrower is wise to wait. The borrower's credibility would be significantly damaged if the loan officer were to learn that the company's invoices were past due.

Categorized organization of information will permit the loan officer to absorb as much or as little information as needed. The format suggested below accommodates further evaluation and consideration in the loan review process.

Does the Borrower Need A Business Plan?

How do companies use business plans? Too often borrowers put a business plan together only when seeking to borrow money from lenders or investors. Business plans should provide information on the short-term strategies for accomplishing long-term goals. Business plans should detail how the human resources will convert the marketing, operational, and financial resources into a successful venture. Business plans should be used to measure results against projections.

Many people are obsessed with business plans, particularly those who charge exorbitant fees to prepare them. Business plans are good, even necessary, in many situations (such as for a start-up business operation); but they are over-used in many instances. When an existing business is seeking to obtain additional financing, a business plan can be a duplication of efforts, considering the documentation requirements of the lender.

If a business plan is contrived merely to justify financing, then it has limited utility or value for the borrower or the lender. If the loan officer requires a business plan, then the borrower should justify the investment of time by producing a plan which will benefit the business and which will be reviewed annually to evaluate past results and to reaffirm future goals.

This chapter outlines at least 95% of all possible information which could be requested for a commercial loan - information that is more pertinent and detailed than is usually included in any business plan. While describing the contents of a business plan targeted to obtain a business loan, this chapter further suggests a format preferred by most lenders.

Borrower Beware!

Many loan officers have had the unfortunate experience of entering into discussions with a borrower who was using false, exaggerated, or misleading information to obtain credit. Whether or not the ploy succeeded, the effects are often felt by legitimate borrowers, whose applications are scrutinized with even more suspicion due to the experience. While loan officers are usually diligent to confirm as much information as possible about potential borrowers, there is a natural inclination toward trusting people with whom one conducts business.

Unless actual loan losses have been incurred, most lenders may be hesitant to prosecute loan applicants found to have used false information to obtain their loan. The federal government is not so hesitant. The Inspector General's Office of the Small Business Administration is available to investigate any attempts to defraud the SBA with false or misleading information. These cases are prosecuted by Office of the U.S. Attorney, which has unlimited resources to perform its job. Federal prosecutors have over a 90% success rate of conviction.

For those individuals who are flippant about the integrity of their business dealings, or who willingly try to obtain an SBA loan with fraudulent information, these actions can carry heavy penalties. It is a federal crime to submit false information in order to induce a lender and the SBA to provide business financing, which could result in criminal prosecution, civil fines, and denial of future participation. Conviction of such an offense is punishable by imprisonment for as many as twenty years and by a fine of as much as $1,000,000.

Borrowers certify the accuracy and completeness of the information they submit in the SBA Business Loan Application. This covenant acknowledges that the information is provided by the borrower in order to obtain loan approval. Borrowers also affirm that they have not made payments to anyone within the government for assistance with the loan application, nor will they hire anyone employed by the agency for a period of two years after the loan is approved.

In 1994, the SBA began to verify each borrower's personal and business income tax returns with the Internal Revenue Service. There have been many instances of fictitious tax returns submitted to the agency by fraudulent loan applicants, resulting in significant loan losses. The SBA now confirms that the income tax returns submitted to the lender and to the agency conforms to the income tax returns which were submitted to the IRS for income tax reporting purposes.

Business Loan Proposal

The borrower should produce information addressed to the lender which clearly sets forth the exact loan proposal being requested by the borrower. At a minimum, this information should included the following components:

General Information

Loan Purpose	Loan Justification	Use of Proceeds
Application Form	Collateral Information	Requested Loan Structure

Personal Administrative Information

Date of Birth	Social Security Number	Place of Birth
Citizenship	Current/Previous Address	Regulatory Questions
Military Record	Spouse Information	Other Business Interests

Business Administrative Information

Business Name	Address	Taxpayer ID
Date Established	Number of Employees	Name of Bank
Previous SBA Debt	Lease Agreements	Business Indebtedness
Business Owners	Regulatory Questions	Business History
Organizational Chart	Key Employee Resumes	Credit Authorization

For Corporations:	Articles of Incorporation	By-laws
	Corporate Seal	Corporate Resolution
	List of Corporate Officers	Certificate of Good Standing

For Partnerships:	Partnership Agreement	List of Partners
	Certificate of Good Standing	Certificate as to Partners

Financial Information

Personal Financial Stmt.	Personal Tax Returns	Business Financial Stmts.
Interim Financial Stmt.	Net Worth Reconciliation	Fin. Stmt. Analysis
A/R Aging	Inventory Aging	A/P Aging
Business Tax Returns	Financial Projections	

Collateral Information

Real Property Collateral

Legal Description	Appraisal	Property Description
Survey	Location Map	Engineering Reports
Environ. Report	Environ. Questionnaire	Photographs
Lease Agreements	Sales Contracts	

Personal Property Collateral

Description	Manufacturer	Cost
Date Acquired	Serial Numbers	Location
Appraisal	Photographs	Price Quotations

Automotive Collateral

Description	Manufacturer	Date Acquired
Cost	Serial Numbers	Mileage (or log hours)
Registration No.	Title	Appraisal
Photographs		

Securities Collateral

Brokerage Statements	Schedule of Closely-held Securities

Notes Receivable Collateral

Description	Name of Debtor	Balance of the Note
Interest Rate	Repayment Terms	Collateral
Current Status	Collateral Values	Copy of Notes

Depository Account Collateral

Description	Name of Depository	Name on Account
Type of Account	Account Balance	Interest Rate on Account
Maturity of Account	Account Statements	

Accounts Receivable / Inventory Collateral

A/R Aging	Bad Debt Schedule	Inventory Aging
Obsolete Inventory	Inventory Valuation	Borrowing Base Certificate
Customer Lists		

Cash Surrender Value Collateral

Copy of Policy	Policy Declaration	Assignment Form

Marketing Information

What Are the Products or Services of the Business?
How Does the Business Operate?
Who Buys the Products or Services?
How Does the Business Advertise?
Who Is the Competition?
How Will the Borrower Increase Revenues?

Miscellaneous Information

Affiliates

Year End Financial Statement	Interim Financial Statement

Construction Loans

Performance Bonds	AIA Contract	Cost Breakdown
Boundary Survey	Sealed Construction Plans	Construction Specifications
Addendum	Soil Reports	Construction Schedule
Curb Cut Permits	Building Permit	Insurance
Utility Letters	Zoning	Alternates

Franchise Businesses

Franchise Information	Franchise Agreement	Franchise Disclosure

Special Assets

Contracts	Lottery Awards	Trusts
Tax Exempt Bonds		

SBA Documents

Business Loan App.	Stmts Required By Law	Stmt of Financial Need
Stmt of Per. History	Compensation Agreement	Compl. for Nondiscrimination
Certif. for Debarment	IRS Request for Transcript	

A detailed discussion of each of these documentation requirements is contained in the following pages. If any of the recommended items are not applicable to the borrower's business or loan request, disregard it when compiling this information.

General Information

Purpose of the Business Loan - The lender wants a concise statement of exactly why the borrower wants to borrow money. It is important to provide the lender with an explanation of the purpose of the loan and where all of the funds will be spent. Do not be surprised if the loan officer is not satisfied with the borrower's statement of merely wanting to purchase an asset.

The loan officer will require a greater explanation as to what the borrower is seeking to accomplish with that asset. The borrower may want to buy a new fork lift, for the purpose of that purchase is to increase productivity in warehouse operations, by lowering labor costs and reducing the exposure to job-related injuries. It is important for the loan officer to understand the costs savings which will effectively pay for the fork lift.

Justification of the Business loan - The borrower is wise to produce a statement of how a business loan is the best source of the funds being requested. The lender may be aware of alternative sources for the financing, and will want to test whether the borrower has considered them as well.

The borrower should be prepared to explain why this loan is the most advantageous source of financing, due to lower costs, better terms, higher leverage, or other parameters which made the borrower choose to apply for the loan with this lender.

Be specific as to how the borrower has chosen the equity contribution proposed for the borrower to invest in the transaction. If there is a logical reason to limit the company's investment, identify it to the loan officer. Otherwise, be prepared for the loan officer to be insistent that the borrower contribute a minimum sum into the transaction.

Proposed Structure of the Loan - The borrower should propose to the lender how the loan would be structured, at the time the loan request is submitted. Loan structure refers to the definition of the transaction between the lender and borrower, including the specific conditions under which funds are provided.

The borrower has the best opportunity to influence these conditions at the beginning of negotiations. By introducing the borrower's preferred conditions up front, the borrower sets the tone for discussions, and is likely to get a better deal, than if the borrower allowed the lender to unilaterally decide on the loan terms.

If the borrower fails to be specific about the loan structure, the loan officer will define these terms without any input from the borrower. The loan officer will structure the loan based solely on what is best for the lender's advantage, sometimes without sufficient input as to what the borrower wants, needs or can afford.

Loan officers sometimes do not appreciate the borrower's desire to provide for cash contingencies, which can be assisted by borrowing extra funds, repaying over longer terms, and of course, using lower interest rates. Be assured that when the loan officer chooses to structure the deal, the borrower risks getting terms that are either too little, too soon, too high, or all of these combined.

Be reminded that the lender will always have the ultimate leverage in determining the loan terms. But, the borrower's suggestion of reasonable terms in the proposal is an important communication to the lender which sets the tone for the loan negotiations. Components of the loan structure should include:

- *Loan Amount* - Specify exactly how much money the borrower wants, and be ready to defend it with other information included in this section.

- *Loan Term* - Define the period over which the borrower requests to repay the loan.

- *Interest Rate* - Although any suggestion is probably of little or no consequence in this category, suggest what appears to be an appropriate interest rate for the transaction.

It is not necessary or wise to initiate negotiation about the structure of the proposed loan until the loan officer has reviewed most of the borrower's application, and provided a definitive expression of confidence that the lender will approve the loan. Any discussions of loan structure prior to that time could be rendered moot, or be subject to further negotiation based on subsequent information which may come to the attention of the loan officer.

Be sure to know the mechanics of calculating a loan payment, based on the amount, interest rate, and repayment term, before initiating negotiating about the loan structure. Being able to accurately calculate the probable loan payment is essential for the borrower, so that it can set limitations as to what can be acceptable or unacceptable. There is no sense in agreeing to terms in which the borrower does not have the capability of performing.

There are several financial software programs which provide loan amortization formulas such as Lotus 123 or Excel. Or, the borrower may choose to invest in a $30 business calculator to accomplish this task.

Use of Loan Proceeds - The borrower's business loan proposal must include a specific schedule which defines how the proceeds of the loan will be used. If the borrower does not specifically declare exactly how much is needed, the loan officer may decide instead, which could be disastrous for both parties.

The loan officer will want and deserve to know precisely where every dollar goes. When the borrower is purchasing an asset, this number is easy to define. But, if the borrower seeks to borrow a portion of the funds for working capital, detailing where these funds will be applied is a little trickier.

For working capital financing, the borrower should produce a fairly detailed month-to-month cash flow projection, predicting how and when the working capital proceeds will be used, and describe the reasonably expected expenses or purchases which will be paid. It is easier to restrict the use of those proceeds to larger ticket items, such as inventory, contracted services, or other costs directly related to the cost of goods sold, which can be identified without as much documentation.

Documenting the Use of Proceeds - The borrower should produce accurate documentation which details how the funds will be spent. The SBA requires varying degrees of such documentation, including copies of any notes being refinanced along with the appropriate security agreements, land purchase or construction contracts, bills of sale, price quotations for assets being purchased, or other specific documents which back up the costs claims.

If there is working capital in the transaction, prepare a schedule of where these funds will be applied. If the borrower is also financing the transaction costs, seek assistance from the loan officer to determine exactly what these costs will be.

Collateral - The borrower should define what is believed to be reasonable collateral to secure the loan, but be aware of the importance the loan officer will place on this loan condition. Collateral is very important to the loan officer because it usually defines their tangible alternative to the normal liquidation of a loan. The lender will typically require coverage for 100% of the loan, with assets valued on a discounted basis.

For example, if the borrower is purchasing a building with the loan proceeds, the loan officer will discount the value the property in order to determine a collateral value. If the lender's loan policy defines an advance rate of 75% on commercial real estate, the lender will reduce the value of the borrower's real property by 25% to determine the collateral value. On that basis, the lender will lend the borrower up to 75% of the cost of the building.

Should the borrower need a loan of a greater sum to cover closing expenses or other business costs, the lender will require the borrower to pledge additional assets in order to secure this loan in excess of its policy limitations.

Most lenders margin real estate at 75%, but that figure varies depending on the loan policy of each specific lender, and the condition of the local real estate market. Unimproved real estate is usually margined at 50%.

Lenders generally value equipment and furniture at 50% of cost, and give little or no value to leasehold improvements or fixtures. Accounts receivable and inventory (the company's "current assets") are subject to valuation determined by what the borrower sells, to whom the borrower sells it, and according to what terms.

However, recognize that these current assets have very little value, if any, to the lender unless these assets are regularly monitored by the lender. Unmonitored current assets can disappear too fast to be considered dependable collateral for a lender.

Loan Application Form - Some lenders require that the borrower submit a loan application form that is unique to the lender. This application is not to be confused with the SBA Business Loan Application. Many lenders choose to use an in-house application form which requests the same information from the borrower.

This document is probably used by the lender as an internal document to move the loan request through its loan approval process, or for loading the approved loan onto its loan accounting system. The borrower should just be patient, and be prepared by inquiring whether the lender requires such a form be completed during the process. The information already gathered can be completed on this form to allow the borrower to move on to more important parts of the application being prepared.

Special Information - If there are special circumstances, negative or positive, which affect the borrower's access to financing. these circumstances should be presented to the loan officer at an early stage of the application process. With increasing frequency, borrowers have extraordinary conditions which require special handling by the loan officer on a case-by-case basis.

During the past several years, thousands of persons with great character and impeccable credit have encountered conditions beyond their control which have tarnished otherwise perfect financial records. The unpredictable economy, some unavoidable bankruptcies, and soaring divorce rates have damaged thousands of borrowers while not necessarily reflecting their character, or capability to repay a loan.

Lenders will discover these conditions early during their due diligence procedures, so it is better for the borrower to introduce the topic, and provide an explanation. This voluntary discussion relieves any suspicion from the loan officer of an attempt by the borrower to hide this information, and provides a legitimate forum from which to shape the loan officer's interpretation of any such events.

Get the loan officer interested in the deal first, with the information described earlier in this chapter. Inclusion of this special information at this stage of the loan proposal permits the loan officer to react early in the process, and facilitates a direct dialog about the situation.

There is more detailed discussion about different circumstances which may have been experienced by borrowers in Chapter Four. Information in Chapter Four suggests how the borrower might approach the loan officer with this information in light of the business loan application.

Personal Administrative Information

The lender will require personal information about each party guaranteeing the proposed loan, and each individual who owns an interest in the business entity. This information is designed to assist the lender, and the SBA by ensuring that the individual is eligible for SBA participation.

The information serves as a declaration of certain facts which may or may not be available from other sources, but is pertinent to the borrower's capability of obtaining SBA financing. Certain information may also result in further review by other government agencies.

Specifically, if the borrower or any of its owners have been convicted of a crime, other than minor traffic offenses, SBA regulations require an FBI review to insure that the borrower has completed all sentencing requirements. Prior conviction of a felony does not deem an individual ineligible for SBA financing. But all terms of the sentencing must have been completed, including probation, in order for financing to be considered.

The information required on each individual involved includes:

Date of Birth - Federal law prohibits a person's age from being used as a qualification (or disqualification) for obtaining a loan. The individual's date of birth is used as a verification of identification.

Social Security Number - This number is required for identification purposes.

Place of Birth - This information is required to confirm citizenship.

Declaration of Citizenship - The individuals are required to declare their country of citizenship. If any individual is not a U.S. citizen, proof of citizenship must be provided, and the alien status of the individual disclosed, with appropriate documentation.

Current Home Address, and Occupancy Dates - This information is required as per SBA regulations.

Previous Home Address, and Occupancy Dates - This information is required as per SBA regulations.

Declaration of Military Service - This information is required as per SBA regulations.

Name of Spouse and Spouse Social Security Number - This information is required as per SBA regulations.

List of Business Interests in Which You Own 20% or More - This information is required as per SBA regulations to determine the eligibility of the borrower. If any such interests exists, it is necessary to produce a recent financial statement for each such business.

Regulatory Questions *(with a written response required to answer any affirmative replies)*:

- Are you presently under indictment, on parole, or probation?

- Have you ever been charged with or arrested for any criminal offense other than a minor motor vehicle violation?

- Have you ever been convicted, placed on pretrial diversion, or placed on any form of probation including adjudication withheld pending probation, for any criminal offense other than a minor motor vehicle violation?

- Have you ever been involved in bankruptcy or insolvency proceedings?

- Are you involved in any pending lawsuits?

- Do you or your spouse or any member of your household, or anyone who owns, manages, or directs your business or their spouses or members of their households work for the Small Business Administration, Small Business Advisory Council, SCORE or ACE, any Federal Agency, or the participating lender?

Most of this information is required to complete the SBA Form 4 (the Business Loan Application), and Form 912 (the Statement of Personal History), which are found on Illustration 3-H and 3-J, respectively.

Business Administrative Information

The lender will require administrative information about the borrower in order to evaluate the proposed loan. This information is designed to assist the lender, and the SBA by ensuring that the borrower is eligible for SBA participation.

The information serves as a declaration of certain facts which may or may not be available from other sources, but is pertinent to the borrower's capability of obtaining SBA financing. It also provides the lender with information from which the lender can determine how the lender is organized, and the depth of the borrower's human resources.

Registered Business Name - The loan officer needs to know the exact legal name under which the business is legally registered, along with any trade names or d/b/a (i.e., doing business as...) under which the company operates. This principally applies to corporations or partnerships, since sole proprietorships are not required to register their name as a legal entity.

Address of the Business - The loan officer will need to know the exact mailing address and principal location of the business, as well as a list of any other offices, stores, plants, warehouses, or other sites used by the business in the course of normal operations. Also the principal telephone number of the business.

Taxpayer Identification Number *(T.I.N.)* - Loan officers request this information for verification of the business, and for identification purposes.

Date Established - The borrower should be able to define the date on which the business was established.

Number of Employees - The lender will require that the borrower define how many persons the company employs, including all affiliated businesses, and subsidiaries. In addition, the borrower will be requested to estimate the number of employees which will be added by the borrower if the proposed financing is approved. This information may be necessary to ensure the borrower's eligibility.

Name and Address of Principal Bank - The lender will requests to know the name and address of the principal depository bank used by the borrower.

Previous SBA/Government Debt - The borrower must disclose any previous loans requested or obtained through the SBA or other Federal agencies, the amount, the date of request, whether or not it was approved, what the current balance is, and what the current status is of the loan.

Name and Address of Any Professionals Assisting The Borrower's Efforts - If the borrower is using any professional assistance for the preparation of the SBA application, this fact must be disclosed to the SBA, along with an estimate of any fees being paid for these services.

Schedule of Business Indebtedness - The borrower must provide a schedule of business loans and debts, which should balance with the most recent interim financial statement submitted by the borrower.

List of Business Owners - The lender needs a complete list of the individual owners of the business, with names, social security numbers, addresses, and their respective percentage of ownership. In addition, the SBA requests to know whether the individuals named completed any military service (along with the period of service stated), and which racial and gender classifications describe the individuals.

Regulatory Questions *(with a written response required to answer any affirmative replies):*

- Has any officer of the business ever been involved in bankruptcy or insolvency proceedings?

- Is the business involved in any pending lawsuits?

- Does the business own a 20% or more interest in other businesses?

- Does the business presently engage in Export Trade?

- Does the business intend to begin exporting as a result of this loan?

History of the Business - The lender can better understand the business if the borrower can document a history of the business. The borrower should provide a detailed narrative which discusses the founding of the company, and some of the highlights which have been accomplished during the period the business has operated.

Relevant information would include the growth of company in terms of revenues, locations, employees, and profitability. This section should detail the products or services offered by the company, the market in which the company seeks to address, and the company's competition.

Organizational Chart - This document will provide a graphic demonstration which defines the business entity's chain of command, or lines of authority. It is important to the lender to understand the flow of authority and the various positions used by the company to accomplish its mission.

List of Key Employees - The loan officer can gain more confidence in the borrower, and the borrower's plans, if the lender has information concerning the key persons within the organization who will contribute to the company's efforts. This information should provide details which cannot be included on the organizational chart, and provides the specific functions of each person, as they relate to the borrower's operation.

In larger transactions, particularly with long term repayment, the loan officer will be concerned about executive management succession, which can be addressed with this information.

Resumes of Borrowers and Key Employees - This information supports the organization chart and list of key employees with a detailed description of the capabilities of the key employees of the borrower. This information quantifies the level of competence the borrower has in form of human capital to accomplish its mission. If possible, this information should be prepared in a standard format, with each resume prepared in the same layout and style. This makes the information easier to read, compare, and interpret.

Credit Authorization - The borrowers should provide the lender with written authorization to obtain a credit report about each owner, shareholder, or partner who will be guaranteeing the requested loan. An example of such an authorization can be found on Illustration 3-A.

The credit report is intended to disclose to the loan officer the past credit history of the individuals. This information is needed in order for the lender to determine whether the individuals have satisfactorily performed with their other creditors, or whether there are unresolved problems which could interfere with the lender's confidence or ability to be repaid. The credit report also reveals if there are any matters of public record regarding an individual, such as judgments, tax liens, bankruptcies, or debts under collection.

Lease Agreements - If the borrower occupies leased premises, the lender will require a copy of the borrower's lease agreement. This requirement covers every building occupied by the business. The lender will expect that the borrower's lease not expire before, or lease have an option to renew for a period extending to, the maturity of the loan.

Illustration 3-A

AUTHORIZATION TO RELEASE INFORMATION

TO: _____ (the "Lender")

This document grants the Lender the authority to investigate and verify my bank account information, deposit balance(s), employment information, and credit history; to obtain a consumer or business credit report; to make any other inquires pertaining to my qualifications for the requested loan; and authorizes the recipient of this document to release to the Lender any and all information that may be requested by the Lender for the purpose of considering my application for a credit transaction. This document may be reproduced to acquire references from more than one source and any reproduction will have the same effect as the original document.

NAME_____ S.S. #_____

DATE OF BIRTH_____/_____/_____

HOME ADDRESS

_____

_____

_____

City   State   Zip Code

_____   _____
             SIGNATURE   DATE

SPOUSE INFORMATION (if spouse has any ownership in business enterprise)

NAME_____ S.S. #_____

DATE OF BIRTH_____/_____/_____

_____   _____
             SIGNATURE   DATE

Business Organization Documentation - The loan officer needs documentation which describes whether the borrower has established a legal entity under which to conduct business. There are three primary legal structures to organize a commercial business, including a sole proprietorship, a partnership, and a corporation.

If the borrower is operating as a sole proprietorship, this fact simply means that a separate legal entity has not been created for the business enterprise. Therefore, the business is operating as an individual, without any additional administrative information required than what is requested of the borrower personally.

If the business is organized as a **Corporation**, the following documentation is required, which provides certain information about the corporation:

> • *Articles of Incorporation* - This document is used in most states to register a corporation with each state's authority which registers business entities (the Secretary of State in most states), to be legally recognized in that state as a corporate entity. The Articles are usually stored with the company's organizational documents, in the corporate minute book, or with the company's attorney.

> • *By-laws* - This document sets forth the official rules which govern the corporation. The By-laws should be adopted by the corporation at the time it is incorporated. The By-laws are also usually filed with organizational documents, in the corporate minute book, or with the company's attorney.

> • *Corporate Seal* - Most states require that a corporation have a seal, which is a stamping device which produces a distinctive imprint of the corporation's name on documents. Lenders often require corporate borrowers to use their corporate seal on particular application documents in order to confirm the corporate authority of any signer.

> • *Corporate Resolution* - The loan officer will request a corporate resolution confirming that the borrower's Board of Directors has authorized the corporation to enter into negotiations for the proposed loan. SBA Form 160 can be used for this requirement. A copy of this form can be found on Illustration 3-B.

• *List of Corporate Officers* - The loan officer will require a list of corporate officers (those persons within the corporation who hold a legal position as defined in the By-laws, and an brief description of their specific responsibilities within the organization.

• *Certificate of Good Standing* - The lender will require corporate borrowers to produce a certificate of good standing, issued by the state authority which regulates businesses (the Secretary of State in most states). This certificate provides an up-to-date confirmation that the corporation is officially recognized by the state and authorized to conduct business.

If the business is a **Partnership**, the following documentation is required, which provides certain information about the partnership:

• *Partnership Agreement* - The loan officer will require that the borrower to provide a copy of the partnership agreement, and any amendments or attachments which may have modified that agreement.

• *List of Partners* - The loan officer will require that the borrower provide a complete list of the partners which is representative of 100% ownership of the partnership. This list should provide the names, addresses, respective percentage of ownership, and status of partnership interests (general or limited). This information should also describe the specific duties which each partner manages for the business entity.

• *Certificate of Good Standing* - The lender will require partnership borrowers to produce a certificate of good standing, issued by the state authority which regulates businesses (the Secretary of State in most states). This certificate provides an up-to-date confirmation that the partnership is officially recognized by the state and authorized to conduct business.

• *Certificate as to Partners* - The borrower should provide the lender with a Certificate as to Partners, which is a signed authorization attesting the authority of the partnership to apply for and enter into an agreement for the loan. At a minimum this certificate will be signed by each general partner in witness of a notary public. SBA Form 160A can be used for this requirement. A copy of this form can be found on Illustration 3-C.

Illustration 3-B

OMB APPROVAL NO. 3245-0201
Expiration Date: 12-31-87

SBA LOAN NO.

(For Corporate Applicants)

U.S. Small Business Administration
RESOLUTION OF BOARD OF DIRECTORS OF

_____
(Name of Applicant)

(1) RESOLVED, that the officers of this corporation named below, or any one of them, or their, or any one of their, duly elected or appointed successors in office, be and they are hereby authorized and empowered in the name and on behalf of this corporation and under its corporate seal to execute and deliver to the _____
(hereinafter called "Lender") or the Small Business Administration (hereinafter called "SBA"), as the case may be, in the form required by Lender or SBA, the following documents: (a) application for a loan or loans, the total thereof not to exceed in principal amount $_____, maturing upon such date or dates and bearing interest at such rate or rates, as may be prescribed by Lender or SBA; (b) applications for any renewals or extensions of all or any part of such loan or loans and of any other loans, heretofore and hereinafter made by Lender or SBA to this corporation; (c) the promissory note or notes of this corporation evidencing such loan or loans or any renewals or extensions thereof; and (d) any other instruments or agreements of this corporation which may be required by Lender or SBA in connection with such loans, renewals, and /or extensions; and that said officers in their discretion may accept any such loan or loans in installments and give one or more notes of this corporation therefore, and may receive and endorse in the name of this corporation any checks or drafts representing such loan or loans or any such installments;

(2) FURTHER RESOLVED, that the aforesaid officers or any one of them, or their duly elected or appointed successors in office, be and they are hereby authorized and empowered to do any acts, including but not limited to the mortgage, pledge, or hypothecation from time to time with Lender or SBA of any or all assets of this corporation to secure such loan or loans, renewals and extensions, and to execute in the name and on behalf of this corporation and under its corporate seal or otherwise, any instruments or agreements deemed necessary or proper by Lender or SBA, in respect of the collateral securing any indebtedness of this corporation;

(3) FURTHER RESOLVED, that any indebtedness heretofore contracted and any contracts or agreements heretofore made with Lender or SBA on behalf of this corporation, and all acts of officers or agents of this corporation in connection with said indebtedness or said contacts or agreements, are hereby ratified and confirmed;

(4) FURTHER RESOLVED, that the officers referred to in the foregoing resolutions are as follows:

_____	_____	_____
(Typewrite name)	(Title)	(Signature)
_____	_____	_____
(Typewrite name)	(Title)	(Signature)
_____	_____	_____
(Typewrite name)	(Title)	(Signature)
_____	_____	_____
(Typewrite name)	(Title)	(Signature)

(5) FURTHER RESOLVED, that Lender or SBA is authorized to rely upon the aforesaid resolutions until receipt of written notice of any change.

CERTIFICATION

I HEREBY CERTIFY that the foregoing is a true and correct copy of a resolution regularly presented to and adopted by the Board of Directors of _____at a meeting duly called and held at _____
(Name of Applicant)

on the_____ day of _____ 19,_____ , at which a quorum was present and voted, and that such resolution is duly recorded in the minute book of this corporation; that the officers named in said resolution have been duly elected or appointed to, and are the present incumbents of, the respective offices set after their respective names; and that the signatures set opposite their respective names are their true and genuine signatures.

(Seal)

Secretary _____

SBA Form 160 (11-85) REF: SOP 50 10 EDITION OF 11-67 WILL BE USED UNTIL STOCK IS EXHAUSTED
* U.S. Government Printing Office 1986-619-370/40191

TSoft Financial Software, Inc. © 1994 - 199

Illustration 3-C

OMB Approval No. 3245-0201
Expiration Date 12-31-87

SBA Loan Number

U.S. Small Business Administration
Certificate as to Partners

We , the undersigned, are general partners doing business under the name and style of_____.

_____ and

constitute all partners thereof. Acts done in the name of or on behalf of the firm, by any one of us shall be binding on said firm and each and all of u

This statement is signed and the foregoing representations are made in order to induce the _____

_____(hereinafter called "Lender") or the Small Business.

Administration (hereinafter called "SBA"):

1. To consider applications for a loan or loans to said firm when signed by any one of us.
2. To make a loan or loans to said firm against a promissory note or promissory notes signed in the firm name by any one of us.
3. To accept as security for the payment of such note or notes any collateral which may be offered by any one of us.
4. To consider applications signed in the firm name by any one of us, for any renewals or extensions for all or any part of such loan or loans and any other loan heretofore or hereafter made by Lender or SBA to said firm.
5. To accept any other instruments or agreements of said firm which may be required by Lender or SBA in connection with such loan, renewals, or extensions when signed by any one of us.

Any indebtedness heretofore contracted and any contracts or agreements made with Lender or SBA on behalf of said firm and all acts of partners or agents of said firm in connection with said indebtedness or said contracts or agreements are hereby ratified and confirmed, and we do hereby certify that THERE IS ATTACHED HERETO A TRUE COPY OF OUR AGREEMENT OF PARTNERSHIP.

   Each of the undersigned is authorized to mortgage and/or pledge all or any part of the property, real, personal or mixed, of said firm as security for any such loan.

This statement and representations made herein are in no way intended to exclude the general authority of each partner as to any acts not specifically mentioned or to limit the power of any one of us to bind said firm and each and every one of us individually.

Lender or SBA is authorized to rely upon the aforesaid statements until receipt of written notice of any change.

Signed this_____ day of _____, 19_____

(Typewrite Name)	(Signature)
(Typewrite Name)	(Signature)
(Typewrite Name)	(Signature)
(Typewrite Name)	(Signature)
(Typewrite Name)	(Signature)
(Typewrite Name)	(Signature)
(Typewrite Name)	(Signature)

State of _____)

County of _____) SS:

On this _____ day of_____ 19_____before me personally appeared.

_____ and _____ and _____ and

_____ and _____ and _____ and

_____ and _____ and _____

be known to be the persons described in and who executed the foregoing instrument, and acknowledged that they executed the same as their free act and deed.

_____
Notary Public

My Commission expires _____

NOTE: If this form of notarial certificate cannot be used in the State in question, the form should be properly modified.

SBA Form 160A (12-87)   TSoft Financial Software, Inc. © 1994 - 1995

Financial Information

The lender will require financial information about the borrower in order to evaluate the proposed loan. This information is designed to assist the lender, and the SBA by ensuring that the borrower is eligible for SBA participation.

The information serves as a declaration of certain facts which may or may not be available from other sources, but is pertinent to the borrower's capability of obtaining SBA financing. It also provides the lender with information from which the lender can determine how the lender is performing, and the prospects of future success.

Personal Financial Statements - The loan officer will require a personal financial statement from every business owner, and from any other party which may be prepared to personally guarantee the business loan. The personal financial statement is intended to provide the lender with an accurate statement of the assets, liabilities, income, and other pertinent financial information concerning these individuals.

Individuals often submit inaccurate financial information, which either understates or overstates their financial information. Most such submissions are made due to the individual's confusion or lack of understanding of the financial statement. Some individuals try to inflate their financial statements in order to appear to be a more qualified borrower to the lender, but these efforts are usually easy to recognize.

There are many standard financial statement forms available from most lenders, and one is available from the SBA, which is the preferred form on which to submit this information. A copy of the SBA Form 413 (the Personal Financial Statement) is found on Illustration 3-D.

In order to clarify questions which may arise in preparing the personal financial statement, be mindful of the following guidelines:

   • Establish a date of the report, and describe the various asset and liability accounts in terms of their approximate value. Round figures to whole dollars, and for simplicity, consider rounding entries to the nearest $100.

   • This report is not considered an audit, so every entry is not going to be examined to verify that it balances to the penny. But know that the loan officer can spot exaggerations, and will question the borrower about any entries that seem out of context.

• Liquid asset accounts (cash, accounts receivable, marketable securities, etc..) should be listed according to the latest balance the depositor can document. If the lender is depending on the borrower using cash, or selling securities to produce an equity contribution to the business, they may ask for written proof of the deposit accounts or brokerage account balances listed on the financial statement.

• Real estate, automobiles, and other major fixed assets should be valued at the likely market value, or the price at which they could be sold in a reasonable amount of time. The financial statement will provide space for greater detail about the real estate assets, such as the address, the names in which the property is titled, its date of purchase, its purchase price, the estimated market value, and the present mortgage balance. This additional information is in recognition that real estate usually comprises a majority of most individual's net worth.

• The borrower should remember to place a value on any closely-held stock or partnership interests owned, particularly in the subject business entity. These assets should be valued according to the percentage of ownership, based on a reasonable assessment of the market value of the company.

• Borrowers should make an entry under "Other Assets" to reflect the cost or value of household and personal assets which have been acquired such as furniture, art, silverware, jewelry, furs, antiques, silver, etc.. The loan officer will not verify or seek to use these assets to secure the loan, but including a reasonable value for these assets on the financial statement insures that any consumer debt which may have been used to purchase these assets is offset. These asset figures are a relevant statement of the accumulation of personal assets.

• Borrowers should segregate liabilities into distinct categories, including bank notes (i.e. car loans, personal notes, and student loans), credit cards/retail accounts (i.e. Visa, Master Card, Discover, Sears, Penneys, and Macys), and real estate debt (any debt which mortgages the borrower's real property, including equity lines of credit).

Illustration 3-D

OMB Approval No. 3245-0188

PERSONAL FINANCIAL STATEMENT

U.S. SMALL BUSINESS ADMINISTRATION

As of _____

Complete this form for: (1) each proprietor, or (2) each limited partner who owns 20% or more interest and each general partner, or (3) each stockholder owning 20% or more of voting stock or (4) any other person or entity providing a guaranty on the loan.

Name	Business Phone
Residence Address	Residence Phone
City, State, & Zip Code	
Business Name of Applicant/Borrower	

ASSETS	(Omit Cents)	LIABILITIES	(Omit Cents)
Cash on hands & in Banks	$ _____	Accounts Payable	$ _____
Savings Accounts	$ _____	Notes Payable to Banks and Others . . . . (Describe in Section 2)	$ _____
IRA or Other Retirement Account	$ _____	Installment Account (Auto).	$
Accounts & Notes Receivable	$ _____	Mo. Payments $	
Life Insurance-Cash Surrender Value Only (Complete in Section 8)	$ _____	Installment Account (other) . . . . . Mo. Payments $	$ _____
Stocks and Bonds . . . . . (Describe in Section 3)	$ _____	Loan on Life Insurance	$ _____
Real Estate . . . . (Describe in Section 4)	$ _____	Mortgages on Real Estate . . . . . (Describe in Section 4)	$ _____
Automobile - Present Value	$ _____	Unpaid Taxes . . . . . (Describe in Section 6)	$ _____
Other Personal Property (Describe in Section 5)	$ _____	Other Liabilities . . . . . (Describe in Section 7)	$ _____
Other Assets . . . . (Describe in Section 5)	$ _____	Total Liabilities	$ _____
		Net Worth	$ _____
Total . . $ _____		**Total** . . $ _____	

Section 1. Source of Income		Contingent Liabilities	
Salary	$ _____	As Endorser or Co-Maker	$ _____
Net Investment Income	$ _____	Legal Claims & Judgments	$ _____
Real Estate Income	$ _____	Provision for Federal Income Tax . . .	$ _____
Other Income (Describe below)*	$ _____	Other Special Debt	$ _____

Description of Other Income in Section 1.

*Alimony or child support payments need not be disclosed in"Other Income"unless it is desired to have such payments counted toward total income.

Section 2.   Notes Payable to Bank and Others.   (Use attachments if neccesary. Each attachment must be identified as a part of this statement and signed).

Name and Address of Noteholder(s)	Original Balance	Current Balance	Payment Amount	Frequency (monthly, etc.)	How Secured or Endorsed Type of Collateral

SBA Form 413 (2-94) Use 5-91 Edition until stock is exhausted. Ref: SOP 50-10 and 50-30 TSoft Financial Software, Inc. © 1994 - 1995

Illustration 3-D Cont.

Section 3. Stocks and Bonds
(Use attachments if necessary. Each attachment must be identified as a part of this statement and signed).

Number of Shares	Name of Securities	Cost	Market Value Quotation/Exchange	Date of Quotation/Exchange	Total Value

Section 4. Real Estate Owned.
(List each parcel separately. Use attachments if necessary. Each attachment must be identified as a part of this statement and signed).

	Property A	Property B	Property C
Type of Property			
Address			
Date Purchased			
Original Cost			
Present Market Value			
Name & Address of Mortgage Holder			
Mortgage Account Number			
Mortgage Balance			
Amount of Payment per Month/Year			
Status of Mortgage			

Section 5. Other Personal Property and Other Assets
(Describe, and if any is pledged as security, state name and address of lien holder, amount of lien, terms of payment, and if delinquent, describe delinquency).

Section 6. Unpaid Taxes.
(Describe in detail, as to type, to whom payable, when due, amount, and to what property, if any, a tax lien attaches).

Section 7. Other Liabilities
(Describe in detail).

Section 8. Life Insurance Held.
(Give face amount and cash surrender value of policies - name of insurance company and beneficiaries).

I authorize SBA/Lender to make inquiries as necessary to verify the accuracy of the statements made and to determine my creditworthiness. I certify the above and the statements contained in the attachments are true and accurate as of the stated date(s). These statements are made for the purpose of either obtaining a loan or guaranteeing a loan. I understand FALSE statements may result in forfeiture of benefits and possible prosecution by the U.S. Attorney General (Reference 18 U.S.C. 1001).

Signature: _____ Date: _____ Social Security Number: _____

Signature: _____ Date: _____ Social Security Number: _____

PLEASE NOTE: The estimated average burden hours for the completion of this form is 1.5 hours per response. If you have questions or comments concerning this estimate or any other aspect of this information, please contact Chief, Administrative Branch, U.S. Small Business Administration, Washington, D.C. 20416, and Clearance Office, Paper Reduction Project (3245-0188), Office of Management and Budget, Washington, D.C. 20503.

TSoft Financial Software, Inc. © 1994 - 1995

• The borrower is usually requested to subtract the total liabilities from the total assets to determine the net worth of the individual.

• If income is requested, estimate the annual income from primary sources of income. Other sources of income, such as real estate, dividends, distributions, interest, or consulting, should be listed separately on an annualized basis.

• The lender usually wants to be informed of any contingent liabilities of the individuals, which may include anticipated taxes, fines, guaranteed or co-signed obligations, or other special debts which are not direct obligations as of the date of the financial statement.

• Any asset or liability entry which needs explanation should be listed in specified sections on page two. These sections are where borrowers can provide information to the lender before the inevitable questions are asked. Also there is generally a section requesting specific information about life insurance on the individual. The information requested includes the insurer, the amount of coverage, the named beneficiary, the cash surrender value, if any, and the named assignee, if any.

• Be sure to sign and date the financial statement. The individual's social security number is usually required in order to verify identification.

Copies of Personal Income Tax Returns - The loan officer will request that individuals submit copies of their income tax returns, along with all schedules and applicable attachments for the past three years.   And, in compliance with recent rules enacted by the SBA, the loan officer will require the individuals to authorize the lender to confirm the income tax returns with the IRS. This action is in response to many incidents of fraud where unscrupulous borrowers have used fictitious tax returns to qualify for SBA loans. Borrowers are required to execute an IRS Form 4506 (Request for Copy or Transcript of Tax Form). A copy of this form can be found on Illustration 3-E.

Most CPAs recommend that filers only maintain unsigned copies of income tax returns, since the only signed copy should be the one submitted to the IRS. The loan officer will usually ask that the filer sign the margin of the first page of each income tax return in order to attest to its authenticity. Be sure to place signature away from any signature lines provided on the form, and use a bright colored pen,

Illustration 3-E

Form 4506

(Rev. October 1994)
Department of the Treasury
Internal Revenue Service

Request for Copy or Transcript of Tax Form

Please read instructions before completing form.
Please type or print clearly

SBA
US Small Business Admin.

OMB No. 1545-0429

Note: Do not use this form to get tax account information. Instead, see instructions below

1a. Name shown on tax form	1b First social security number on tax form or employer identification number (See Instructions.)
2a If a joint return, spouse's name shown on tax form	2b Second social security number on tax form

3. Current name, address (including apt., room, or suite no.) city, state, and ZIP code (See Instructions.)

4. If copy of form or a tax return transcript is to be mailed to someone else, show the third party's name and address.

Southeast Capital Associates 5600 Roswell Road Atlanta GA 30342

5. If we cannot find a record of your tax form and you want the payment refunded to the third party, check here . . . . ☐

6 If name in third party's records differs from line 1a above, show name here (See Instructions.)

7 **Check only one box to show what you want:**

a ☐ Tax return transcript of Form 1040 series filed during the current calendar year and the 2 preceding calendar years. (See Instructions.) (The transcript gives most lines from the original return and schedule(s).) There is no charge for a transcript request made before October 1, 1995.

b ☐ Copy of tax form and all attachments (Including Form(s) W-2, schedules, or other forms). The charge is $14.00 for each period requested.
   Note: If these copies must be certified for court or administrative proceedings, see instructions and check here . . . . ☐

c ☐ Verification of nonfilling. There is no charge for this.

d ☐ Copy of Form(s) W-2 only. There is no charge for this. See instructions for when Form W-2 is available
   Note : If the copy of Form W-2 is needed for its state information, check here . . . . ☐

8 If this request is to meet a requirement of one of the following, check all boxes that apply.

☐ Small Business Administration   ☐ Department of Education   ☐ Department of Veterans Affairs   ☐ Financial Institution

9 Tax form number (Form 1040, 1040A, 941, etc.)	11 Amount due for copy of tax form:	
	a Cost for each period	14
	b Number of tax periods requested on line 10	0
10 Tax period(s) (yr. or period ended date). If more than 4, See instructions.	c Total cost. Multiply line 11a by line 11b	0
	Full payment must accompany your request. Make check or money order payable to " Internal Revenue Service"	

Please Sign Here

Signature. See instructions. If other than taxpayer, attach authorization document.   Date

Title (if line 1a above is a corporation, partnership, estate, or trust)

Telephone number of requester

Best time to call

Instructions

A Change To Note. Form 4506 may be used to request a tax return transcript of the Form 1040 series filed during the current calendar year and the 2 preceding calendar years. There is no charge for a tax return transcript requested before October 1, 1995. You should receive it within 10 workdays after we receive your request. For more details, see the Instructions for line 7a.

Purpose of Form -- Use Form 4506 only to get a copy of a tax form, tax return transcript, verification of nonfiling, or a copy of Form W-2. But if you need a copy of your Form (s) W-2 for social security purposes only, do not use this form. Instead, contact your local Social Security Administration office.

Do not use this form to request Forms 1099 or tax account Information, If you need a copy of Form 1099, contact the payer. However, Form 1099 Information is available by calling or visiting your local IRS office.

Note: if you had your tax form filled in by a paid preparer, check first to see if you can get a copy from the preparer. This may save you both time and money.

If you are requesting a copy of a tax form, please allow up to 60 days for delivery. However, if your request is for a tax return transcript, please allow 10 work days after we receive your request. To avoid any delay, be sure to furnish all the information asked for on this form. You must allow 6 weeks after a tax form is filed before requesting a copy of it or a transcript.

Tax Account Information Only -- If you need a statement of your tax account showing any later changes that you or the IRS made to the original return, you will need to request tax account information. Tax account information will list certain items from your return including any later changes.

To request tax account information, do not complete this form. Instead, write or visit an IRS office or call the IRS toll-free number listed in your telephone directory.

If you want your tax account information sent to a third party, complete Form 8821, Tax Information Authorization. You may get this form by calling 1-800-829-3676.

Line1b. -- Enter your employer identification number only if you are requesting a copy of a business tax form. Otherwise, enter the first social security number shown on the tax form.

Line 2b. -- If requesting a copy or transcript of a joint tax form, enter the second social security number shown on the tax form. Note: If you do not complete Line 1b and, if applicable, Line 2b, there may be a delay in processing your request.

Line 3. -- For a tax return transcript, a copy of Form W-2, or for a verification of nonfiling, if your address on line 3 is different from the address shown on the last return you filed and you have not notified the IRS of a new address, either in writing or by filing Form 8822, Change of Address, you must attach either ---

TSoft Financial Software, Inc. © 1994 - 1995

such as blue or red, so that the signature is easy to find and obviously is not copied.

Business Financial Statements - The loan officer will generally request to review the financial statements of the business for the past three years. This information permits the lender to examine the borrower's previous performance, and evaluate the progress made during this period. The loan officer will likely enter the information onto a spreadsheet which allows them to comparatively analyze the financial results from several years.

If practical, the borrower should have its financial statements prepared by a Certified Public Accountant (CPA). This decision is best made by weighing the size of the business against the amount of capital financing being requested. By using an independent professional to report and compile the business financial information, much credibility is added to the financial statements.

There are three general levels of financial reporting:

> • *Compilation* - This financial report has the lowest level of confirmation, since the CPA will merely accept the internally-generated report of receipts and payments, and compile a financial statement based on the appropriate classifications defined by the business. The CPA will correct any blatant errors which may be discovered, but will typically depend on the client to provide most of the information, which is reported in a generally accepted format.

> • *Review* - This financial report is prepared by compiling the financial information, and then testing several categories to assure accuracy. The CPA accepts a greater responsibility in issuing a review statement, and is obligated to report all inconsistencies found the accounting methods or in the preparation of financial statements. Further, the CPA confirms to the company's owners that the information has been prepared consistent with Generally Accepted Accounting Principles (GAAP).

> • *Audit* - This financial report is the highest level of financial reporting, where the CPA prepares the financial statement after testing every revenue and expense classification and confirming the validity of all balance sheet entries. The report is issued with an opinion of the CPA as to its accuracy, disclosing any exceptions or inconsistencies.

74

There are no standards as to when a business should use one financial accounting report or another. This decision should be made based on the particular needs of the business, and who is expected to receive the information. A compilation is fine for a company with $20 million in sales if there is only one shareholder who does not plan to borrow any money. However, a company with sales of $3 million desiring to make a public offering must have three years of audited financial statements.

The loan officer should inform the borrower which level of financial reporting is preferred by the lender. If there are have several shareholders, or it is anticipated that the company's borrowing requirements will exceed $500,000, it is a good idea to get a review-level financial report. The review statement will provide sufficient credibility of the company's financial position, without the high cost of audit.

Recognize that the financial statements of the business are probably the most important portion of the application which determines whether or not the borrower will qualify for financing. The quality of its preparation therefore is germane to the company's ability to obtain a loan. Many businesses utilize an in-house bookkeeper to organize their financial records, and produce a basic financial statement for operations. This information is usually the basis for the work performed by the company's CPA, at the appropriate reporting period.

Many companies pay for a CPA to prepare a monthly compiled financial statement. Such an effort is usually a waste of money, unless required by the lender, or if an absentee owner wants an independent report of the monthly financial results. A small business generally will not need an independently prepared financial statement more than once per quarter.

Loan officers will require a borrower's financial report to be submitted to the lender on at least an annual basis, as of the last day of the company's fiscal year. Regardless of the type of financial statement prepared for the company, it should be completed within ninety days after the end of the reporting period. Often, loan covenants will request this information within sixty days, but the borrower should make a point to allow ninety days if this financial report is prepared by a CPA. It usually requires that long to prepare.

Interim Financial Statement - The lender will require that the loan application include an interim financial statement which is no more than 90 days old. This information is particularly important during the last half of the year, when more time will have passed since the previous year end report. The need for this interim report is prompted by an SBA requirement that each loan guaranty application be submitted with updated interim financial statements.

Reconciliation of Net Worth - Provide the loan officer with a reconciliation of net worth, if needed. Often, there are adjustments made to the retained earnings, or other accounts within the equity portion of the balance sheet. These adjustments are not always obvious, and can distract the loan officer attempting to analyze the financial statements. Prepare this reconciliation ahead of time and provide a detailed explanation of any miscellaneous changes or adjustments.

Analysis of Financial Statements - It is beneficial for the borrower to provide the loan officer with a detailed narrative of the business financial reports, describing each specific reporting period. This analysis permits the borrower to influence the loan officer's interpretation of the financial statements, and insure their understanding of any particular nuances of the operating results.

Emphasis should be given to any particular footnotes, adjustments, or events which more favorably explain any negative results, or highlight the positive results. If appropriate, the borrower may even prepare adjusted financial statements to demonstrate the financial results in alternative scenarios, based on relevant events which changed the final results. A number of financial ratios are explained in Chapter Two which may assist the borrower in preparing an analysis for the loan officer's review.

Accounts Receivable Aging Report - The loan officer will request a copy of the accounts receivable aging report, as of the date of the latest interim financial statement. The balance on this report should be equivalent to the accounts receivable balance on the most recently submitted interim financial statement. This information provides the loan officer with an indication of the strength of the company's working capital position.

Inventory Aging Report - If the inventory represents a significant asset for the business, it is helpful to provide the loan officer with an inventory aging report, so that the loan officer can evaluate the components of the company's inventory (raw materials, work-in-process, or finished goods), and the aging of each of these categories. This aging report should be dated, and balance with the inventory balance stated on the most recent financial statement submitted by the borrower.

Also, inform the loan officer of the valuation method used by the company to record the value of inventory. There are two methods by which companies can value the inventory owned by the business:

- First In - First Out (FIFO) - This method values inventory based on the cost of the inventory unit when acquired - that is units are tracked and expensed out as they are used, based on the actual price paid for them when acquired. This method is the more aggressive of the two methods, because it permits the business to retain the higher-valued units on the books while expending the typically lower-cost units. This method results in a higher inventory valuation.

- Last In - First Out (LIFO) - This method values inventory based on the latest cost of inventory units - that is units are expensed out based on the latest market price without regard to the price actual paid for the particular units. FIFO is the more conservative of the two methods because it requires the business to expense the highest price paid for the asset units as they are used, which results in a lower inventory valuation.

Accounts Payable Aging Report - The loan officer will likely request a copy of the accounts payable aging report, as of the date of the latest interim financial statement. The balance on this report should be equivalent to the balance on the most recently submitted interim financial statement. This information provides the loan officer with an indication of the strength of the company's working capital, and how well the company manages its payables .

Copies of Business Income Tax Returns - As with the personal income tax returns, the loan officer will require the business income tax returns with all applicable schedules and attachments, for the past three years. An officer of the company should also sign the margin of the cover page of each income tax return in order to attest its authenticity. Borrowers are required to execute an IRS Form 4506 (Request for Copy or Transcript of Tax Form). A copy of this form can be found on Illustration 3-E.

It is helpful to prepare a separate memorandum to be submitted with copies of the business income tax returns to discuss the tax reporting methods and procedures employed by the business. Many lenders are not very sophisticated in interpreting income tax returns, especially when compared directly to the business financial statements.

Providing information about any unique features of the borrower's tax returns and helping the loan officer reconcile the difference between the tax returns and the financial statements, can reduce questions which inevitably will arise.

The most frequently asked questions concern the differences in financial and tax reporting relate to reconciling retained earnings. While these differences are usually easy to determine through examination of the appropriate tax schedules, sometimes it can be difficult, depending on the degree of detail contained in the tax return. The borrower's preparation of this information makes the loan application review much easier.

Financial Projections - The loan officer will be very interested in the company's projections of financial performance for the periods following the proposed loan. The company's ability to accurately project these figures, or at least justify the basis for these predictions, is an important component in the loan application.

The borrower should prepare the following financial projections to support the loan application:

> • *Balance Sheet Projections* - Using the most recently submitted interim balance sheet, the borrower should demonstrate the immediate effect the loan proceeds would have on the company's balance sheet. This projection is best demonstrated by comparing the pre-loan balance sheet entries to the post-loan balance sheet entries, with appropriate debit and credit entries detailed between the two columns. An example of this projection format is found on Illustration 3-F.

> • *Income Statement Projections* - Based on the existing financial trends and the changes which are expected to result directly from the proposed loan, prepared a detailed income projection of the company for two years. There is additional information about how to develop income statement projections in Chapter Two. An example of an income statement pro forma is found on Illustration 2-A.

> • *Cash Flow Projections* - Using the first year's income projections, prepare a cash flow projection to demonstrate the company's cash cycle on a month-to-month basis. Be sure to show the effect of the loan proceeds during the current period and reflect the principal and interest

Balance Sheet Projections

Business Name: _____

	for the Interim period ending	debits	credits	pro forma balance
ASSETS				
Current Assets:				
Cash	_____	_____	_____	_____
Accounts Receivable	_____	_____	_____	_____
Inventory	_____	_____	_____	_____
Total Current Assets:	$_____			$_____
Fixed Assets:				
Land	_____	_____	_____	_____
Building(s)	_____	_____	_____	_____
Machinery & Equipment	_____	_____	_____	_____
Less: Accum. Depreciation	- _____	_____	_____	- _____
Total Fixed Assets:	_____			_____
Other Assets:				
Intangible Assets	_____	_____	_____	_____
Deposits	_____	_____	_____	_____
Total Other Assets:	_____			_____
Total Assets	$_____			$_____
LIABILITIES & EQUITY				
Current Liabilities:				
Notes Payable - Short Term	_____	_____	_____	_____
Current Maturities - LTD	_____	_____	_____	_____
Accounts Payable - Trade	_____	_____	_____	_____
Accrued Expenses	_____	_____	_____	_____
Total Current Liabilities	$_____			$_____
Long Term Liabilities:				
Long Term Debt	_____	_____	_____	_____
Other	_____	_____	_____	_____
Total Long Term Liabilities	$_____			$_____
Total Liabilities	$_____			$_____
Owner's Equity:				
Stock	_____	_____	_____	_____
Paid-In Capital	_____	_____	_____	_____
Retained Earnings	_____	_____	_____	_____
Total Owner's Equity	$_____			$_____
Total Liabilities & Equity	$_____			$_____

payments of the requested loan as scheduled.

More sophisticated borrowers will even account for revenues generated on a receivable basis, goods purchased on trade credit, and seasonal changes in sales. There is additional information about how to develop cash flow projections in Chapter Two. An example of an month-to-month cash flow pro forma is found on Illustration 2-B.

Collateral Information

It is helpful to the lender - and accelerates consideration of the loan application - if the borrower can provide information about the collateral offered to secure the loan. This data helps the lender assess the collateral value and evaluate the loan proposal. This section outlines a number of items the lender will need to evaluate the specifications of the borrower's collateral, depending on the general nature of the assets.

Generally, the borrower will not have many of these items at the time of loan application, particularly for real property collateral. But any available collateral information can accelerate the loan officer's understanding of exactly how the borrower proposes to secure the loan. Most of this information has to be current or updated if the loan is approved.

There may be a significant difference between the lender's and the borrower's valuation of the collateral assets. Lenders discount the market or cost values of collateral assets when determining the adequacy of collateral against the requested loan total. This discount is justified, since the value of many assets will decrease over time and since the lender has to maintain a financial margin to cover the possible costs of liquidating those assets.

Often the loan officer is clearly too conservative in calculating a prudent advance rate on specific collateral assets. Borrowers can address this issue with information to demonstrate the true value of the assets in question. For example, providing the lender with comparable sales records, advertisements, or other data can establish the value of assets similar to those offered as collateral. This supportive data can give the borrower leverage to negotiate a better allowance for the collateral.

In determining liquidation or collateral value, lenders routinely use the lower of cost or appraised value of an asset as the base from which to discount. But if the borrower is acquiring an asset at a significantly reduced basis and wants to leverage some of the phantom equity thereby created, the borrower should insist that the appraised value be used as the basis from which to determine the collateral values. This method is not unreasonable and does not place any additional risk on the lender. It just challenges the lender's conservative nature which is hesitant to lend money on asset values for which the borrower did not have to pay.

Lenders can require certain collateral, but that does not mean the borrower has to permit them to use it. The borrower can always refuse the lender's offer and try to find a loan somewhere else. **Everything is negotiable**. Most lenders routinely over-secure commercial loans by attempting to encumber virtually every asset owned by the borrower.

The borrower is wise to avoid submitting to the lender's inclination to encumber too much collateral. The lender can be asked to justify everything being sought as collateral; the lender can be asked to defend the valuation of those assets in determining the adequacy of their collateral coverage.

Ultimately, this exercise may not change the lender's requirements, but it may cause the lender to recognize a higher valuation of the borrower's assets. The borrower can sometimes use this position to justify a modification of other requirements of the loan agreement, such as the collateral advance rates and interest rates.

Before entering into serious negotiations for a commercial loan, the borrower should have decided exactly which assets are available and unavailable to pledge as collateral. In the detailed categories of assets described below, some suggestions are made concerning their suitability and exposure as collateral. There are recommendations about how to manage some of the situations the borrower may face if certain assets are requested as collateral.

If unwilling to pledge a certain asset as collateral, the borrower should not be forced through economic pressure. Instead, the borrower can employ creative negotiations to tighten the lender's approach to collateral, reducing the risk of blanket liens most lenders seek on the borrower's assets.

For example, lenders will require a personal guarantee on a commercial loan and require the borrower to post a minimum of 100% collateral value (on discount-valued collateral). If the loan defaults and the loan officer does not liquidate the assets for the balance of the loan, the lender can still pursue the business owners personally for the balance of the loan.

This situation places an enormous risk on the borrower, given the inexperience of many loan officers in liquidating assets and the piranha-like approach of asset sales conducted by lenders.

The borrower can negotiate limitations on the lender's actions in a liquidation situation by establishing how the lender will sell the assets; Preferably, the lender will agree to allow the borrower to sell the assets, thereby avoiding expensive commissions and set up charges and maximizing the net price. The borrower's cooperation can be very important to the lender. While this topic is unusual to discuss at the loan negotiation stage, it can considerably reduce the risks for both parties.

Depending on the nature of the borrower's collateral being offered, the following information can assist the lender in understanding these assets:

Real Property Collateral - If the borrower chooses to pledge a mortgage interest in a parcel of real property to secure the loan, the following documentation is helpful to evaluate and assess this collateral:

- *Legal Description* - The lender should receive a metes and bounds description of the property, if available, or at least the district and land lot number of the property. This information may be found on the warranty deed, or mortgages, or it may be attached to the property's purchase contract.

- *Appraisal* - The lender should receive a copy of a current or aged property appraisal on the subject property, if one exists.

- *Description of Property Improvements* - The lender should receive a list of the various improvements on and features of the property which may increase its value (such as extra curb cuts, zoning classifications, and adjacent development).

- *Survey* - The lender should receive a copy of a survey or plat of the property. A survey was probably obtained when the property was purchased. A plat of the property can usually be obtained in the county tax assessor's office.

• *Location Map* - The lender should receive a portion of a local city or county map which depicts the general area containing the property site, including an indication of the exact position of the property.

• *Engineering Reports* - The lender should receive any available engineering studies, especially for older facilities. These reports reflect an engineering inspection of the structure and discussion of the general condition of the structures.

• *Environmental Reports* - The lender should receive any Phase 1, Phase 2, or other environmental inspection reports which may have been previously prepared for the property. If the property contains underground storage tanks (USTs), the lender should be given copies of any testing or inspection results of the UST.

• *Environmental Questionnaire* - The borrower should be prepared to assist the lender with the completion of the Environmental Questionnaire and Disclosure Statement that details pertinent information about real property which will secure the loan. If the property has never been used for commercial or agricultural purposes, there may be sufficient grounds for the lender to waive the requirement of a Phase 1 Survey based on the responses to this questionnaire. A copy of this form can be found on Illustration 3-G

• *Photographs* - The lender should receive photographs of the property and its improvements. Visualization of the property can reinforce the loan officer's recognition of the value of the asset.

• *Lease Agreements* - The lender should receive copies of leases for tenants who occupy part or all of the subject property. The lender may give the borrower credit for the income generated from renting portions of the property, but the SBA will not recognize that income - the borrower must generate sufficient income from operations to repay its debt. This rule is necessary since the SBA cannot finance an investment property operation, which would be the source of such income.

Illustration 3-G

Environmental Questionnaire and Disclosure Statement Required
When Other Real Estate is Pledged as Collateral

For all other real estate pledged as collateral but not purchased from loan proceeds, the following Environmental Questionnaire and Disclosure Statement must be completed:

Address and Legal Description

_____

_____

_____

1. Are you aware of any previous uses of the site that may have posed a threat to its environment integrity? ☐ Yes ☐ No

2. To the best of your knowledge, has disposal or accidental release of any hazardous substance ever occurred at the site? ☐ Yes ☐ No

3. Are you aware of any pollution clean-up actions that have ever been taken at this site? ☐ Yes ☐ No

4. Are toxic chemicals stored or utilized at the site? ☐ Yes ☐ No

5. Are hazardous wastes generated at the site that may require an EPA identification number? ☐ Yes ☐ No

6. Are you aware of any underground storage tanks that are located on the site? ☐ Yes ☐ No

7. As far as you know, is the site currently in violation of any federal, state, or local hazardous substance regulations? ☐ Yes ☐ No

8. Other_____

_____
Applicant/ Borrower

_____
Date

_____
Title

If the answer to any of the above questions is YES, a Phase I Environmental Risk Report will be require

Environmental Risk Reports as required will be prepared at the expense of the Borrower by persons whose qualifications are acceptable to the Lender and SBA.

• *Sales Contracts* - If the borrower is acquiring the subject real property as part of the total transaction, the lender should receive a copy of the executed sales contract.

Concerning Personal Residences - A frequent conflict arises between lenders and borrowers concerning the lender's requirement that individual business owners encumber their personal residences. The lender justifies this requirement by seeking to secure the personal guaranty of the business loan. Sometimes the equity value of the individual's residence is needed to provide adequate collateral for the loan, but sometimes this equity is not needed.

If the transaction requires the personal equity to secure the loan, the borrower may have to choose whether to pledge the house or pass on the loan commitment. If the individual is married, the spouse is usually a 50% co-owner of the residence and will have to consent to any such encumbrance.

If the transaction does not require the individual's residential equity in order to provide sufficient collateral for the loan, then the lender is seeking "psychological collateral." This collateral position is intended to remind borrowers of their personal commitment to insuring the lender that the loan will be repaid. While the SBA rarely forecloses on a personal residence, that is the ultimate risk of allowing the lender to place a mortgage on it.

The lender and the SBA want the borrowers to provide some assurance that repayment of the loan will be a high priority with them, regardless of the success of the business operations. Lenders also want to protect their position in the individual's net worth. A personal guaranty can be worthless if unsecured. The individual can obtain additional financing which could lead to other lenders with claims against the unencumbered equity in the personal residence.

This requirement has killed many transactions, because some borrowers are simply not willing to meet this condition. It is a business decision which has to be faced when obtaining small business financing.

There are some strategies to employ in attempting to convince the lender to waive or modify the requirement of using an individual's personal residence as collateral. These suggestions may or may not be applicable, depending on the situation of the individuals:

- The borrower can offer to substitute other assets not previously requested by the lender to replace the personal residence collateral requirement.

- The borrower can explain to the loan officer that the spouse will absolutely not permit such an encumbrance. This position may prove to be an effective negotiating ploy if the equity is not needed to fully secure the loan.

- The borrower can offer to pledge a 50% undivided interest in the personal residence. This scenario reduces the individual's exposure, limiting the borrower to having a 50% partner in the residential property.

- Before the loan application begins, the borrower can execute a quit claim deed to the spouse for the 50% interest in the personal residence. Because the individual then can legally and morally exclude the residence from the personal financial statement, the lender cannot require it as collateral. This tactic carries a number of potential legal and tax consequences, and should be considered only after careful evaluation and counsel from an attorney and CPA.

- If the residential equity is not needed to fully secure the loan, the borrower can sometimes get the lender to agree that, upon successful completion of three or four years of loan payments, the lender will release the mortgage against the personal residence. This compromise will demonstrate a good faith effort on both parties to accommodate this sensitive requirement.

Sometimes the borrower will have to agree to this requirement in order to obtain the business loan. In fact, most small business owners have pledged their residences against business financing at one time or another. If the house has a large first mortgage, it is not likely that the business lender would ever foreclose on the house and take on another large obligation of the individual's.

The borrower need not be concerned about the risks of personal financial planning involved with a second lien on the residence. During periods of dropping residential interest rates, most lenders will accommodate a refinance of a residence if it will save the borrower money. The lender will generally agree to subordinate to the new lender or cancel the second lien, so long as the individual executes a new lien to keep the lender in the same position.

Personal Property Collateral - If the borrower chooses to pledge a lien interest in personal property to secure the loan, the following documentation is helpful to evaluate these assets:

- *Description* - The lender should receive a schedule of the personal property assets which includes the following information:

    Asset Description
    Name of Manufacturer
    Date Acquired
    Cost
    Model and Serial Numbers
    Location (if the borrower has more than one location)

- *Appraisal* - The lender should receive a copy of a current or aged appraisal of the subject assets, if one exists. Or, the borrower should assemble relevant quotations of what the assets are currently being marketed for, if this information will demonstrate their relative value.

- *Photographs* - If these assets comprise a major portion of the collateral value to be used by the borrower, the lender should receive photographs of the personal property assets. Visualization of the personal property can reinforce the loan officer's recognition of the value of these assets.

- *Price Quotations* - If the borrower is planning to acquire personal property assets as part of the total transaction, the lender should receive a price quotation which details the costs of the assets being acquired.

Automotive Collateral - If the borrower chooses to pledge a security interest in automotive assets to secure the loan, the following documentation is helpful to evaluate and assess these assets:

- *Description* - The lender should receive a schedule of the automotive assets which includes the following information:

    Asset Description
    Name of Manufacturer
    Date Acquired
    Cost

Model and Serial Numbers
Mileage (or log hours)
State of Registration and License Number

- *Title* - The lender should receive copies of the title of the vehicles, if available.

- *Appraisal* - The lender should receive a copy of a current or aged appraisal of the subject assets, if one exists. Or, the borrower should assemble relevant quotations of what the assets are currently being marketed for, if this information will demonstrate their relative value.

- *Photographs* - If these assets comprise a major portion of the collateral value to be used by the borrower, the lender should receive photographs of the automotive assets. Visualization of the vehicles can reinforcement the loan officer's recognition of the value of these assets.

Securities Collateral - If the borrower chooses to pledge a security interest in listed securities to secure the loan, the following documentation is helpful to evaluate these assets:

- *Brokerage Statements* - The lender should receive copies of recent brokerage account statements or a schedule of the securities portfolio with updated market price quotes if the securities are not held by a brokerage firm. (It is a federal crime to make copies of the share certificates or bonds.)

- *Schedule of Closely-held Securities* - If using closely-held securities as collateral, the borrower should prepare a memorandum describing the securities. This information should include the borrower's valuation and method of valuation, the relative stake of the entity represented by the borrower's securities, and a recent financial statement of the entity. The borrower will be required to deliver the actual securities to the lender at loan closing for safe-keeping during the loan term.

The use of listed securities by the borrower as collateral for a commercial loan is discouraged. The lender will be restricted by Regulation U to value any listed security used as collateral at only 50% of its current market value. Securities priced under $5 per share are generally not accepted by most lenders. And since the lender cannot control the borrower's brokerage account, the lender will have to hold the borrower's bonds or share certificates for safe-keeping during the term of the loan.

These securities cannot be pledged or assigned to another entity or person per se. The borrower is required to actually execute a blank sales receipt to the secured party which is relying on these securities as collateral. Language in most collateral agreements permits the lender to actually initiate a trade of these securities if there is a change in the valuation of the securities which diminishes the lender's collateral position.

That is, the lender can sell the securities and liquidate the loan with the borrower's collateral at any time - regardless of whether the borrower was actually in default or the length of the remaining term. Obviously, this act could have significant tax implications for the borrower.

This requirement can also be very risky for the borrower if the need to trade the securities arises in order to respond to changes in the market value of a specific asset. The lender will become part of that potential decision if the borrower decides to pledge these securities as collateral.

Even if the lender is amenable to working with the borrower in such a scenario, the time required to get the lender's consent or to actually obtain possession of the securities can be delayed. The borrower risks that the lender's decision period can lead to additional market losses (or missed opportunities for the borrower to profit).

Delays in getting possession of the securities can interfere with the borrower's ability to meet the delivery requirements of the rigid securities market. The borrower should not risk its portfolio assets in this manner unless there is a written agreement as to how these situations will be handled.

An alternative is to approach the borrower's brokerage firm for a loan on the borrower's portfolio and the substitute these funds for the portion of the loan which would have been obtained using the securities as collateral. Most major brokerage firms make loans on very reasonable terms against listed securities because they are better positioned to monitor the market changes than other lenders.

The individual security holder should be comfortable with the brokerage firm's ability to make a short-notice margin call. The borrower must understand that these loans are subject to being liquidated quickly if the value of the portfolio falls suddenly.

Notes Receivable Collateral - If the borrower chooses to pledge any notes held in order to secure the loan, the following documentation is helpful to evaluate these assets:

- *Description* - The lender should receive a schedule of any notes held by the borrower or business owners, including the following information:

  Name of Debtor
  Principal Amount of the Note
  Interest Rate
  Terms of Repayment
  Collateral
  Current Status of the Account (current, past due, etc..)

- *Collateral Values* - The lender should receive any information available to identify and justify the value of the collateral.

- *Copy of Notes* - The lender should receive a copy of each note.

Depository Account Collateral - If the borrower chooses to pledge a security interest in a depository account or deposit certificates to secure the loan, the following documentation is helpful to evaluate these assets:

- *Description* - The lender should receive a schedule of all such accounts, including the following information:

  Name of Depository and Name in which the Account is Identified
  Type of Account
  Account Balances
  Current Interest Rate Paid on Account
  Maturity of Each Account

- *Depository Account Statements* - The lender should receive a copy of recent account statements which confirm the balances listed in the schedule.

The borrower should be aware that IRA accounts, Keogh accounts, and 401k accounts are prohibited by law from being used as collateral to secure a loan for any purpose.

Accounts Receivable / Inventory Collateral - If the borrower chooses to pledge a security interest in the current business assets to secure the loan, the following documentation is helpful to evaluate these assets:

- *Accounts Receivable Aging* -The lender should receive a current aging of accounts receivable.

- *Bad Debt Schedule* - The lender should receive a current schedule of bad debts, with an explanation of each account and the borrower's efforts to recover any sums outstanding.

- *Inventory Report* - The lender should receive a current detailed report of the borrower's inventory, segregating raw materials, work-in-process, and finished goods.

- *Obsolete Inventory* - The lender should receive a schedule of the borrower's obsolete inventory and disclosure the borrower's current book value of those assets.

- *Inventory Valuation* - The lender should receive a narrative report detailing how the borrower values the inventory and whether any particular components of the inventory may be subject to volatile price risks.

- *Borrowing Base Certificate* - The lender will require the borrower to prepare and submit a Borrowing Base Certificate at regular intervals. This form is used to define the periodic balances and changes in the borrower's eligible collateral for asset-based loans. This form is usually updated on a daily or weekly basis, depending on the specific arrangement between the lender and borrower.

- *Customer Lists* - The lender should receive a list of the names, addresses, and telephone numbers of the regular customers of the business. The lender needs this information in the event it is ever necessary to attempt to collect the accounts directly from the customers.

Cash Surrender Value - If the borrower chooses to pledge a security interest in the cash surrender value of a life insurance policy held to secure the loan, the following documentation is helpful to evaluate these assets:

- *Copy of Policy* - The lender should receive a copy of the insurance policy which has accrued the cash surrender value being offered as collateral.

- *Policy Declaration* - The lender should receive a recent statement or declaration from the insurance carrier affirming the balance of the policy's cash surrender value;

- *Assignment Form* - The borrower should determine whether the insurance carrier requires a specific document to be executed in order to pledge the proceeds of the cash surrender value of the particular policy. If so, the borrower should obtain it from the insurance company.

Marketing Information

The lender should be provided with marketing information about the borrower to understand what the business contributes to the economy and how the borrower attracts other parties to pay for that contribution. In this category, the borrower defines the business, describes how it is marketed, and details future plans for continuing or expanding the revenue base of the business. This information should be compiled in a marketing summary or even a business plan.

What Are the Products or Services of the Business? The borrower should define exactly what and how products or services are provided by the business. It is easy to understand a company that sells radios, but it takes a greater study to relate to a company that manufactures digitized, variable overdrive power systems.

The lender should be told what the borrower does with those products or services. Does the borrower manufacture, distribute, retail, resell, liquidate, remodel, recover, research, or re-manufacture the products? If the company sells services, is it providing research, information, analysis, advice, or solutions?

The lender should be able to completely understand what specific niche the borrower serves and what particular market the business addresses. And if the borrower can distinguish business as unique, the lender should be able to understand why the business is discernibly different from the competition in the market.

How Does the Business Operate? The loan officer should be given an idea as to how the business operates. After defining the products or services, the borrower should explain how the business uses them, sells them, manufactures them, or provides them. In addition, the borrower should explain the logical sequence of events that defines the normal course of the business operation. Again, the purpose is to educate the loan officer about what the borrower does, so that the loan officer can be more responsive to what the borrower wants to do.

For example, the loan officer needs to understand that it takes the borrower twenty minutes to prepare, fry, and glaze ten dozen doughnuts, but the borrower can sell fifteen dozen doughnuts in twelve minutes. With this perspective, the loan officer will appreciate why the borrower wants to acquire a larger capacity to produce doughnuts.

Who Buys the Products or Services? Two of the most important management tools available to a business owner are knowing who the customer is and who the customer can be? This information is crucial in the design of the product or service, pricing, business location, capability to perform, and strategic planning to determine and achieve the business goals.

By sharing this information with the loan officer, the borrower communicates strength as a manager. In addition, this information supports the request for financing because it will give the lender confidence that the borrower understands the dynamics of the market in which the company operates.

How Does the Business Advertise? Included in the loan application package should be a description of the ways in which the borrower markets and advertises the business. There is not necessarily a right or wrong way to raise awareness about the business, but explaining the activities and media through which the borrower promotes the business provides more credibility for the operation.

The lender should receive copies of any print ads, flyers, brochures, specialty products, or other tangible items which have been distributed to advertise the business. The borrower can also produce a detailed report about media advertising, such as radio, television, cable, yellow pages, billboards, or signage.

Also important are the civic organizations, trade associations, community activities, contributions, sponsorships, youth sports leagues, fundraising events, and other involvements through which the borrower has promoted the business.

Who Is the Competition? Identify the other businesses which provide the same products or services and which are trying to attract the same customers. The borrower should be honest in assessing the competitor's strengths, weaknesses, and advantages. The borrower should be specific about the position of each competitor in the market. In explaining where the borrower stands in comparison, the borrower can describe the plan to maintain or increase market share. The lender needs to know the unique features of the market the borrower is operating within and the opportunities which the borrower sees there.

How Will the Borrower Increase Revenues? Some of the most important information the borrower can give to the lender is a marketing plan to describe how the business will increase its revenues. If the loan proposal is to provide additional assets or capital to directly increase revenues, the borrower has to support that proposal with a plan detailing exactly how such increases will be accomplished.

The financial projections will provide a numerical measure of the revenue increases the borrower predicts, but the marketing plan has to define the basis for those predictions. In order words, the borrower has to relate to specific numerical increases by describing what causes them. If the loan enables the borrower to make twenty more dozen doughnuts per hour and the borrower can sell these doughnuts for eight hours at $3.00 per dozen, it stands to reason that the revenues will increase by $480 per day, or $14,400 per month.

This detailed explanation and reasoning lends credibility and rationality to the borrower's financial projections. The process of dissecting and describing the correlation between the marketing efforts and financial results also communicates to the lender that the borrower understands the operational capabilities and limitations of the business.

Miscellaneous Information

Many categories of information are going to relate specifically to the borrower's particular situation, depending on the nature of the business or purpose of the loan.

Several of these categories of information are included in this section. Listed here in alphabetical order, they should be used if the business situation applies to them.

Affiliates - Affiliated companies affect a borrower's participation in the SBA loan guaranty programs. Affiliates are defined as any other business entity in which the borrower, or any holder of at least 20% of the borrower's business, own at least a 20% interest. The affiliated companies are considered collectively with the enterprise which the borrower is seeking to finance for purposes of determining eligibility under the SBA loan guaranty program.

That is, any and all business interests in which the borrower and any of the borrower's partners or shareholders, individually or collectively, own at least a 20% stake, are considered along with the entity seeking to borrow money. The purpose is to determine the total sales, number of employees, net income, or net worth to compare to the eligibility limitations for obtaining a loan guaranty.

The lender will be required to confirm the borrower's eligibility if affiliated companies exist, so the borrower should be prepared to provide the lender with the following information. This documentation will be provided to the SBA as well.

- *Year End Financial Statement* - The most recent year end financial statement of each affiliated company.

- *Interim Financial Statement* - The most recent interim financial statement, if the year end statement provided is more than 90 days old at the time this information is forwarded to the SBA.

If eligibility is subjected to close scrutiny due to the relative size of any affiliate, it may be necessary to provide the past two years of financial statements in order to permit the lender to average the statements, as provided for in the regulations.

Construction Loans - Borrowers seeking to obtain financing for the construction of improvements to real property will be required to have an additional layer of documentation. These documents are specifically intended to satisfy the lender that the business risks are not compounded by any extraordinary risks associated with the construction aspect of the transaction.

The format of a normal construction loan requires the lender to make an initial advance of loan proceeds for the purchase of real property (if necessary) and to make additional draws on an "as completed" basis. In other words, the lender will provide the borrower with enough funds to pay for 20% of the construction costs after 20% of the construction is completed.

This type of lending carries additional risks due to the involvement of a third party who is responsible for the management of the construction project. The building contractor has to get the project started and keep the project moving between the draws of borrowed funds. Contractors use either their own working capital or the borrower's equity which is advanced through the lender.

In addition, the contractor has to be able to complete the project for the predetermined amount, or the borrower could run short of funds without having a completed building. With the advent of new building standards, zoning codes, and environmental regulations, the lender must be diligent in insuring that the proposed structure will be constructed in compliance with all applicable laws.

Most lenders wisely use a construction consultant who specializes in monitoring projects to administer the lender's construction loan. This consultant will review the pertinent information before the loan closes in order to assure the lender that the project is feasible, is in compliance with applicable laws, and can be completed within the approved financing.

After loan closing, the consultant will monitor the progress of the project and inspect the site when the contractor requests a loan draw. This inspection will determine whether the contractor has made sufficient progress on the structure to justify the requested loan advance, in accordance with the agreed upon terms governing the lender's construction loan. By working strictly for the lender, the consultant protects the lender's interest on the project site.

The extraordinary risk faced by the borrower and lender is that the financial condition of the contractor can create serious problems if the contractor cannot keep the project going between loan draws. A stalemate occurs if the contractor draws all of the loan funds available, but cannot pay for labor or materials necessary to get to the next stage of the project.

If the borrower is seeking construction financing, the lender will likely require that the borrower provide the following documentation in order to close the loan, or at least before the first loan draw is approved. References below to the lender may be applicable to the lender's construction consultant, who will supervise the project on behalf of the lender. References to the borrower may be applicable to the contractor, who will likely interface directly with the construction consultant for the transmission of much of this information.

• *Performance and Material Bonds* - Lenders usually will require that the borrower's building contractor provide some form of financial guaranty in order to assure the lender that the contractor's financial condition will not pose a threat to completing the project. This bond, a financial surety given to the lender on behalf of the contractor, insures that funds will be available to complete the project should the contractor's financial condition interrupt the job.

• *Executed AIA Construction Contract* - This contract is a widely accepted standard to define the expectations and requirements of a contractor. It should be submitted with *any and all attachments, amendments, or addendum*, in order for the lender to know the complete agreement and specifications agreed to by the borrower and the contractor. Most lenders require the borrower to enter into these contracts with at least a 10% retainage allowance. The borrower is able to accrue up to 10% of the total amount owed under the contract until final inspection of the project has been approved by the lender.

• *Cost Breakdown* - The lender will require a schedule of values, which defines each component of cost assigned by the contractor for the project. This information is relevant on either a contracted price or cost plus contract. It permits the lender to test the reliability of the contractor's estimates for the cost of completing the project.

• *Boundary Survey* - The lender will require a boundary survey to show the parameters of the property and will want to see exactly where the building is to be built. This survey should also demonstrate compliance with local set-back lines and denote any easements on the property.

• *Complete Set of Sealed Construction Plans* - The lender will require the borrower to provide a full set of blueprints imprinted by the architect. In evaluating the project, the lender and the consultant will compare these plans with the other information that has been submitted.

• *Complete Set of Construction Specifications* - The lender will require the borrower to provide a full schedule of specifications.

- *Complete Set of Addendum* - The lender will require the borrower to provide a full set of any plan or specification addendum which have been added to the project.

- *Complete Set of Alternates* - The lender will require the borrower to provide a full set of any alternates permitted under the project plans or specifications.

- *Soil Reports* - The lender will require the borrower to provide copies of any soil tests completed on the site for the purpose of evaluating the percolation, compression, or contamination.

- *Construction Schedule* - The lender will require the borrower to provide the construction schedule agreed upon between the contractor and borrower. By confirming that the construction schedule conforms to the term of the proposed loan schedule, the lender can monitor progress after construction begins.

- *Curb Cut Permits* - Where applicable, the lender will require the borrower to provide copies of any curb cut permits which have been obtained from the appropriate government subdivision.

- *Building Permit* - The lender will require the borrower to provide a copy of the building permit which has been obtained from the appropriate government subdivision.

- *Proof of Insurance* - The lender will require the borrower to provide a declaration of insurance form confirming that the contractor has liability, workers compensation, and builder's risk insurance. This insurance has to name the lender as the additionally insured, with written notice required to the lender prior to cancellation.

- *Utility Letters* - The lender will require the borrower to provide copies of letters obtained from various utility companies, confirming to the borrower that these utilities have agreed to furnish their services to the subject property. At a minimum, these letters should be obtained from the providers of electricity, natural gas, telephone service, water and the sanitary/storm sewer.

• *Zoning Letter* - The lender will require the borrower to provide a copy of a letter from the appropriate government subdivision responsible for zoning, confirming the zoning code of the subject property and defining the specific use permitted on the property.

Franchise Businesses - Many small business owners choose to affiliate with franchised businesses. There are many advantages to this strategy, such as the access to proprietary products, methods, and services for the business to sell. Also name recognition in the public marketplace is easier to promote with the backing of a national organization. Although all of these advantages come with a price, franchised businesses generally have a lower failure rate than non-franchised businesses.

If the borrower is seeking to finance a franchised business, the lender will need the following information in order to precede with the loan request:

• *Information on Franchisor* - The lender will want to be familiar with the franchisor, particularly with lesser known one which may not yet have national recognition. The lender should be given the informational brochures and marketing materials which the borrower received in selecting the particular franchisor.

• *Franchise Agreement* - The lender will require a copy of the borrower's signed Franchise Agreement, including all attachments and exhibits. The lender needs to know how the franchisor operates in the event of a possible disposal of the borrower's franchised operation. Determining which party would control the continued use of the trade name, proprietary equipment, and methods directly affects the franchise's value to the lender as collateral and the lender's risk in dealing with the specific franchisor.

• *Franchise Disclosure Statement* - The Federal Trade Commission requires franchisers to publish a disclosure report to provide the franchisee with specific operational and financial information about the franchisor and its management. This report is intended to protect prospective buyers from receiving dishonest or fraudulent information from unscrupulous franchise operators or sales representatives. A copy of this report should be submitted to the lender for review and a second opinion.

Special Assets - Some borrowers possess certain assets which require extraordinary consideration when offered as collateral for a proposed loan.

Although there is no asset that assures the borrower of loan approval, some assets definitely strengthen the chances of loan approval. Lenders relish the opportunity of lending money which is obtainable even if not readily accessible.

These special assets might include any of the following categories detailed below. Included here are suggestions about how borrowers might use such assets to obtain business loans. For any of these options, the borrower should insist that the lender provide financing at a lower interest rate, since the nature of the asset will assure the lenders repayment.

The borrower should seek advice from an attorney before executing any documents pledging these kinds of assets to a lender. (With common assets, such as real property or equipment, the Uniform Commercial Code provides the lender with standard language, forms, and precedent to perfect the lender's interest in the borrower's assets.) When pledging these special assets, a custom agreement will be written to provide for the lender's security. The borrower's attorney must be involved to protect the borrower's interests in a situation where lenders and their attorneys probably have very little experience. Failure to evaluate such an agreement adequately could lead the borrower to granting rights to the lender which could prove disastrous in the event of default.

The borrower must insure that the lender's liquidation of the loan would be conducted in a specified manner. Liquidation should not threaten the future value of these special assets nor create unnecessary that damage the residual value of the asset after the loan has been satisfied.

- *Contracts* - One special asset is the long-term payout provisions of a deferred contract to which the borrower has satisfied the obligation. Common for former sports professionals, this type of asset is also being seen as the settlement for a job buyout from many Fortune 1000 companies. The contracts often guaranty the recipient a fixed sum to be paid out over a specified term, insuring an income stream over that period.

- *Lottery Awards* - As more states and sales promotions utilize lotteries, there are more winners. Most of the major awards provided in these contests are paid out over a twenty-year period and can be assigned to a third party.

- *Trusts* - Many persons have the benefit of a trust that has been established to administer either an inheritance or a large financial settlement. These trusts specify to whom, under what conditions, and when the proceeds are to be distributed to the beneficiary.

Unless prohibited by the trust, the income stream can generally be assigned to a third party. The lender will need assurances that there are no special conditions which could alter or cease the income stream. Usually, the corpus assets of the trust cannot be pledged to a third party. This situation may not be true for smaller trusts or for those with a limited number of beneficiaries.

- *Tax Exempt Bonds* - Many tax-exempt securities cannot be used as collateral because they are restricted from third party assignment by the issuer. However, the income stream and final proceeds of the matured securities can be pledged by the holder. The trustee of the bond issuer can be directed to send interest payments and principal proceeds to any party designated by the beneficiary. This arrangement effectively allows the beneficiary to use the corpus of these investments to secure a commercial loan.

SBA Documents

Depending on how active the borrower's lender is in the SBA program, the borrower may be as familiar with SBA documents as the lender. The application for a loan guaranty is typically prepared by the lender or a consultant engaged either by the lender or the borrower. Although the SBA loan application has a bad reputation, it is not really very complicated.

Lenders who process a relatively high volume of SBA guaranteed loans, may have software which produces SBA approved application documents. Lenders who do not handle many SBA loans may be struggling to manually prepare a seemingly intimidating set of forms, with many unfamiliar pages and blanks.

The application consists of relatively few SBA forms. It is the additional information required to accompany these SBA application forms that seem to create a lot of work for the borrower and lender. The challenge for the lender is to determine the exact set of information needed for a specific transaction before it is submitted to the SBA. No two loans are alike.

There is an advantage to the borrower drafting and providing the basic SBA application documents to the lender together with the loan proposal. The borrower benefits by providing the requested information in a format which the lender will have to use. Optional by recommended, this presentation can save the lender some work and will hopefully decrease the time required to process the application.

If the lender does not process many SBA applications, the borrower's assistance can be particularly helpful. The lender may actually utilize the documents the borrower prepares, if typed neatly. Whether or not the borrower chooses to complete these documents, it is helpful to understand the purpose of each document, and the information being requested.

The following documentation comprises a standard SBA loan guaranty application:

> • *Form 4 - Application for Business Loan* - This SBA form contains much of the basic information requested on the business, including a proposed allocation of the loan proceeds, a detailed schedule of the existing business liabilities, and covenants bounding the borrower to specific SBA rules and regulations. A copy of this form can be found on Illustration 3-H.
>
> Most of the additional information requested to support the loan proposal is defined as an exhibit to this document and is intended to accompany the application when submitted to the SBA. Detailed earlier in this chapter these items include:
>
> Exhibit A   -   Schedule of Collateral
>
> Exhibit B   -   Personal Financial Statement (Form 413 - see Illustration 3-D)
>
> Exhibit C   -   Business Financial Statements for the past three years, including balance sheet, profit and loss statement, and reconciliation of net worth; also an interim financial statement no more that 90 days old, with a current aging of accounts receivable and accounts payable; also earnings projections for at least two years.

Exhibit D	-	Statement of History of the Business
Exhibit E	-	Resumes on the business managers and owners
Exhibit F	-	Names, social security numbers, and personal financial statements of any identified guarantors
Exhibit G	-	List of any equipment to be acquired with loan proceeds, and name and address of seller
Exhibit H	-	Details of any bankruptcy proceedings of any company officers
Exhibit I	-	Details of any pending lawsuits involving the business
Exhibit J	-	Names and addresses of any related parties employed by the SBA, a federal agency, or the lender;
Exhibit K	-	Details of any affiliated interests (20% or more) of the owners of the business applicant, along with recent financial statements on their affiliated entities
Exhibit L	-	Details of any related party from which the business applicant regularly buys products or services, or to which the business applicant regularly sells products or services
Exhibit M	-	For franchised business applicants, a copy of the franchise agreement and the FTC disclosure statement
Exhibit N	-	Estimated construction costs and a statement of the source of any additional funds
Exhibit O	-	Preliminary construction plans and specifications

Illustration 3-H

OMB Approval No. 3245-0016
Expiration Date: 6-30-94

U.S. Small Business Administration
APPLICATION FOR BUSINESS LOAN

Individual	Full Address

Name of Applicant Business

Full Street Address of Business	Tel. No. (inc. A/C)	Tax I.D. or SSN

City	County	State	Zip	Number of Employees (Including subsidiaries and affiliates)
Type of Business			Date Business Established	At Time of Application _____
Bank of Business Account and Address				If Loan is Approved _____
				Subsidiaries or Affiliates (Separate from above) _____

Use of Proceeds: (Enter Gross Dollar Amounts Rounded to the Nearest Hundreds)	Loan Requested		Loan Requested
Land Acquisition	0	Payoff SBA Loan	0
New Construction/ Expansion Repair	0	Payoff Bank Loan (Non SBA Associated)	0
Acquisition and/or Repair of Machinery or Equipment	0	Other Debt Payment (Non SBA Associated)	0
Inventory Purchase	0	All Other _____	0
Working Capital (Including Accounts Payable)	0	Total Loan Requested	0
Acquisition of Existing Business	0	Term of Loan - (Requested Maturity)	_____ 0.000 Years

PREVIOUS SBA OR OTHER FEDERAL GOVERNMENT DEBT: If you or any principals or affiliates have 1) ever requested Government Financing or 2) are delinquent on the repayment of any Federal Debt complete the following:

Name of Agency	Original Amount of Loan	Date of Request	Approved or Declined	Balance	Current or Past Due

ASSISTANCE   List the name(s) and occupations of any who assisted in the preparation of this form, other than applicant.

Name and Occupation	Address	Total Fees Paid	Fees Due
		0	0
Name and Occupation	Address	Total Fees Paid	Fees Due
		0	0

PLEASE NOTE: The estimated burden hours for the completion of this form is 19.8 hours per response. If you have any questions or comments concerning this estimate or any other aspect of this information collection please contact, Chief Administrative Information Branch, U.S. Small Business Administration. Washington D.C. 20416 and Gary Waxman, Clearance Officer, Paperwork Reduction Project (3245-0016), Office of Management and Budget, Washington, D.C. 20503

Illustration 3-H Cont.

ALL EXHIBITS MUST BE SIGNED AND DATED BY PERSON SIGNING THIS FORM

BUSINESS INDEBTEDNESS: Furnish the following information on all installment debts, contracts, notes, and mortgages payable. Indicate by an asterisk (*) items to be paid by loan proceeds and reason for paying same (present balance should agree with the latest balance sheet submitted).

To Whom Payable	Original Amount	Original Date	Present Balance	Rate of Interest	Maturity Date	Monthly Payment	Security	Current or Past Due
Acct. #	$		$			$		
Acct. #	$		$			$		
Acct. #	$		$			$		
Acct. #	$		$			$		

MANAGEMENT (Proprietor, partners, officers, directors all holders of outstanding stock - <u>100% of ownership must be shown</u>. Use separate sheet if necessary.

Name and Social Security Number and Position Title	Complete Address	% Owned	* Military Service From	To	* Race	* Sex

* This data is collected for statistical purpose only. It has no bearing on the credit decision to approve or decline this application.

THE FOLLOWING EXHIBITS MUST BE COMPLETED WHERE APPLICABLE. ALL QUESTIONS ANSWERED ARE MADE A PART OF THE APPLICATION.

For Guaranty Loans please provide an original and one copy (Photocopy is acceptable) of the Application Form, and all Exhibits to the participating Lender. For Direct Loans submit one original copy of the application and Exhibits to SBA.

Submit SBA Form 912 (Personal History Statement) for each person e.g. owners, partners, officers, directors, major stockholders, etc.; the instructions are on SBA Form 912.

If your collateral consists of (A) Land and Building, (B) Machinery and Equipment, (C) Furniture and Fixtures, (D) Accounts Receivable, (E) Inventory, (F) Other, please provide an itemized list (labeled Exhibit A) that contains serial and identification numbers for all articles that had an original value greater than $500. Include a legal description of Real Estate offered as collateral.

Furnish a signed current personal balance sheet (SBA Form 413 may be used for this purpose) for each stockholder (with 20% or greater ownership), partner, officer, and owner. Social Security number should be included on personal financial statement. It should be as of the same date as the most recent business financial statements. Label this Exhibit B.

4. Include the statements listed below: 1, 2, 3 for the last three years; also 1, 2, 3, 4 as of the same date, which are current within 90 days of filing the application; and statement 5, if applicable. This Exhibit C (SBA has Management Aids that help in the preparation of financial statements.) All information must be **signed and dated.**

1. Balance Sheet   2. Profit and Loss Statement.
3. Reconciliation of Net Worth
4. Aging of Accounts Receivable and Payable
5. Earnings projects for at least one year where financial statements for the last three years are unavailable or where requested by District Office.

(If Profit and Loss Statement is not available, explain why and substitute Federal Income Tax Forms.)

5. Provide a brief history of your company & a paragraph describing the expected benefits it will receive from the loan. Label it Exhibit D.

6. Provide a brief description similar to a resume of the education, technical and business background for all the people listed under Management. Please mark it Exhibit E.

Illustration 3-H Cont.

ALL EXHIBITS MUST BE SIGNED AND DATED BY PERSON SIGNING THIS FORM

7. Do you have any co-signers and/or guarantors for this loan? If so, please submit their names, addresses, tax ID Numbers, and current personal balance sheet(s) as Exhibit F.

8. Are you buying machinery or equipment with your loan money? If so, you must include a list of equipment and cost as quoted by the seller and his name and address. This is Exhibit G.

9. Have you or any officer of your company ever been involved in bankruptcy or insolvency proceedings? If so, please provide the details as Exhibit H. If none, check here: ☐ Yes ☐ No

10. Are you or your business involved in any pending lawsuits? If yes, provide the details as Exhibit I. If none, check here: ☐ Yes ☐ No

11. Do you or your spouse or any member of your household, or anyone who owns, manages, or directs your business or their spouses or members of their households work for the Small Business Administration, Small Business Advisory Council, SCORE or ACE, any Federal Agency, or the participating lender? If so, please provide the name and address of the person and the office where employed. Label this Exhibit J. If none, check here: ☐ Yes ☐ No

12. Does your business, its owners or majority stockholders own or have a controlling interest in other businesses? If yes, please provide their names and the relationship with your company along with a current balance sheet and operating statement for each. This should be Exhibit K.

13. Do you buy from, sell to, or use the services of any concern in which someone in your company has a significant financial interest? If yes, provide details on a separate sheet of paper labeled Exhibit L.

14. If your business is a franchise, include a copy of the franchise agreement and a copy of the FTC disclosure statement supplied to you by the Franchisor. Please include it as Exhibit M.

CONSTRUCTION LOANS ONLY

15. Include a separate exhibit (Exhibit N) the estimated cost of the project and a statement of the source of any additional funds.

16. Provide copies of preliminary construction plans and specifications. Include them as Exhibit O. Final plans will be required prior to disbursement.

DIRECT LOANS ONLY

17. Include two bank declination letters with your application. (In cities with 200,000 people or less, one letter will be sufficient.) These letters should include the name and telephone number of the persons contacted at the banks, the amount and terms of the loan, the reason for decline and whether or not the bank will participate with the SBA.

EXPORT LOANS

18. Does your business presently engage in Export Trade?

Check here: ☐ Yes ☐ No

19. Do you have plans to begin exporting as a result of this loan? Check here: ☐ Yes ☐ No

20. Would you like information on Exporting? Check here: ☐ Yes ☐ No

AGREEMENTS AND CERTIFICATIONS

Agreements of non-employment of SBA Personnel: I agree that if SBA approves this loan application I will not, for at least two years, hire as an employee or consultant anyone that was employed by the SBA during the one year period prior to the disbursement of the loan.

Certification: I certify: (a) I have not paid anyone connected with the Federal Government for help in getting this loan. I also agree to report to the SBA office of the Inspector General, Washington, D.C. 20416 any Federal Government employee who offers, in return for any type compensation, to help get this loan approved.

(b) All information in this application and the Exhibits are true and complete to the best of my knowledge and are submitted to SBA so SBA can decide whether to grant a loan or participate with a lending institution in a loan to me. I agree to pay for or reimburse SBA for the cost of any surveys, title or mortgage examinations, appraisals credit reports, etc., performed by non-SBA personnel provided I have given my consent.

(c) I understand that I need not pay anybody to deal with SBA. I have read and understand SBA Form 159 which explains SBA policy on representatives and their fees.

(d) As consideration for any Management, Technical, and Business Development Assistance that may be provided, I waive all claims against SBA and its consultants.

If you make a statement that you know to be false or if you over value a security in order to help obtain a loan under the provisions of the Small Business Act, you can be fined up to $5,000 or be put in jail for up to two years, or both.

If Applicant is a proprietor or general partner, sign below.

By: _____

Date _____

_____

Date _____

_____

Date _____

_____

Date _____

If Applicant is a Corporation, sign below:

_____

Corporate Name and Seal   Date _____

By: _____

Signature of President

Attested by: _____

Signature of Corporate Secretary

Illustration 3-H Cont.

UNITED STATES SMALL BUSINESS ADMINISTRATION
SCHEDULE OF COLLATERAL
Exhibit A

Expiration Date: 6/30/94

Applicant		
Street Address		
City	State	Zip Code

LIST ALL COLLATERAL TO BE USED AS SECURITY FOR THIS LOAN

Section I-- REAL ESTATE

Attach a copy of the deed(s) containing a full legal description of the land and show the location (street address) and city where the deed(s) is recorded. Following the address below, give a brief description of the improvements, such as size, type of construction, use, number of stories, and present condition (use additional sheet if more space is required).

LIST PARCELS OF REAL ESTATE					
Address	Year Acquired	Original Cost	Market Value	Amount of Lien	Name of Lienholder

Description(s):

SBA Form 4 Schedule A (8-91) Use 4-87 edition until exhausted

TSoft Financial Software, Inc. © 1994 - 1995

Illustration 3-H Cont.

SECTION II--PERSONAL PROPERTY

All items listed herein must show manufacturer or make, model, year, and serial number. Items with no serial number must be clearly identified (use additional sheet if more space is required).

Description - Show Manufacturer, Model, Serial No.	Year Acquired	Original Cost	Market Value	Current Lien Balance	Name of Lienholder

All information contained herein is TRUE and CORRECT to the best of my knowledge. I understand that FALSE statements may result in forfeiture of benefits and possible fine and prosecution by the U.S. Attorney General (Ref. 18 U.S.C. 100).

_____   Date _____

_____   Date _____

Statements Required By Law and Executive Order - This statement is an attachment to Form 4 and requires applicants to acknowledge their intention to comply with several federal laws and executive orders. This acknowledgment is documented with the applicant's signature on an attached form.

These particular laws and executive orders include the Freedom of Information Act (5 U.S.C. 552), the Freedom of Financial Privacy Act of 1978 (12 U.S.C. 3401), the Flood Disaster Protection Act (42 U.S.C. 4011), the Executive Orders - Floodplain Management & Wetland Protection (42 F.R. 26951 & 42 F.R. 26961), the Occupational Safety and Health Act (15 U.S.C. 651 et seq.), Civil Rights Legislation, the Equal Credit Opportunity Act (15 U.S.C. 1691), the Executive Order 11738 - Environmental Protection (38 F.R. 25161), the Debt Collection Act of 1982, Deficit Reduction Act of 1984 (31 U.S.C. 3701 et. seq. and other titles), the Immigration Reform and Control Act of 1986 (Pub. L. 99-603), and the Lead-Based Paint Poisoning Prevention Act (42 U.S.C. 4821 et seq.).

This list contains references to several laws with which average citizens may be totally unfamiliar. A summary of each executive order and law is provided with the form so that the borrower can review the specifications before executing the form.

- *Statement of Financial Need* - This document describes the proposed financial transaction, defines the entire costs or expenses involved, and identifies the source of funds for each cost or expense. A copy of this form can be found on Illustration 3-I.

- *Form 413 - Personal Financial Statement* - This document is described earlier in this chapter in the section discussing personal financial information. It is usually included as Exhibit B to the Business Loan Application. A copy of this form can be found on Illustration 3-D.

- *Form 912 - Statement of Personal History* - This document is described earlier in this chapter in the section discussing Personal Administrative Information. A copy of this form can be found on Illustration 3-J.

Illustration 3-I

Statement of Financial Need

	FUNDS PROVIDED BY OWNERS	USE OF LOAN PROCEEDS	TOTAL FUNDS REQUIRED
A. Fixed Assets Acquisition / Repair			
Automotive			$0
Machinery and Equipment			0
Furniture and Fixtures			0
Land			0
Building Construction / Purchase			0
Building Improvements			0
Leasehold Improvements			0
1. Other:			0
2. Other:			0
Total Fixed Asset Acquisition	$0	$0	$0
B. Debt Payment			
Accounts Payable (Attach List)			0
Notes Payable (Complete "Indebtedness" SBA form 4)			0
Total Debt Payment		$0	$0
C. Working Capital			
Operating Cash			$0
Inventory			0
Prepaid Expenses (Attach List)			0
Advertising			0
Deposits (Attach List)			0
Training			0
Accounts Receivable Financing			0
Organizational Costs (Attach List)			0
Other (Specify) Soft Costs			0
1. Other:			0
2. Other:			0
3. Other:			0
Total Working Capital	$0	$0	$0
TOTAL FUNDS	$0	$0	$0

Source of funds provided by owners:

1.

2.

3.

Signature: _____   Date: _____

Illustration 3-J

<table>
<tr>
<td colspan="2">

United States Of America

SMALL BUSINESS ADMINISTRATION

STATEMENT OF PERSONAL HISTORY

</td>
<td>

PLEASE READ CAREFULLY - PRINT OR TYPE
Each member of the small business concern or the development company requesting assistance must submit this form in TRIPLICATE for filing with the SBA application. This form must be filled out and submitted by:

1. If a sole proprietorship by the proprietor.
2. If a partnership by each partner.
3. If a corporation or a development company, by each officer, director and additionally by each holder of 20% or more of the voting stock.
4. Any other person including a hired manager, who has authority to speak for and commit the borrower in the management of the business.

</td>
</tr>
</table>

Name and Address of Applicant (Firm Name) (Street, City, State and ZIP Code)	SBA District/Disaster Area Office
	Amount Applied for: $ 0 Loan Case No.

Personal Statement of: (State name in full, if no middle name, state (NMN), or if initial only, indicate initial). List all former names used, and dates each name was used. Use separate sheet if necessary. First Middle Last	9. Name and address of participating bank Southeast Capital Associates 5600 Roswell Road Atlanta GA 30342
	2. Date of Birth: (Month, day and year)
	3. Place of Birth: (City & State or Foreign Country)

Give the percentage of ownership or stock owned or to be owned in the small business or the Development Company. %	Social Security Number	U.S. Citizen? ☐ Yes' ☐ No If no, give alien registration number:

Present residence address:

From: To: Address:

Home Telephone No (Include A/C):   Business Telephone No. (Include A/C):

Immediate past residence address:

From: To: Address:

BE SURE TO ANSWER THE NEXT 3 QUESTIONS CORRECTLY BECAUSE THEY ARE IMPORTANT.

THE FACT THAT YOU HAVE AN ARREST OR CONVICTION RECORD WILL NOT NECESSARILY DISQUALIFY YOU. BUT AN INCORRECT ANSWER WILL PROBABLY CAUSE YOUR APPLICATION TO BE TURNED DOWN. IF YOU ANSWER "YES' TO 6,7 OR 8, FURNISH DETAILS IN A SEPARATE EXHIBIT. INCLUDE DATES; LOCATION; FINES, SENTENCES, ETC.; WHETHER MISDEMEANOR OR FELONY; DATES OF PAROLE/PROBATION; UNPAID FINES OR PENALTIES; NAMES UNDER WHICH CHARGED; AND ANY OTHER PERTINENT INFORMATION.

Are you presently under indictment, on parole, or probation?
☐ Yes ☐ No   (If yes, indicate date parole or probation is to expire.)

Have you ever been charged with or arrested for any criminal offense other than a minor motor vehicle violation? Include offenses which have been dismissed,
☐ Yes ☐ No   discharged, or nolle prosequi. (All arrests and charges must be disclosed and explained on an attached sheet.)

Have you ever been convicted, placed on pretrial diversion, or placed on any form of probation, including adjudication withheld pending probation, for any
☐ Yes ☐ No   criminal offense other than a minor motor vechicle violation?

☐ Fingerprints Waived ☐ Fingerprints Required Date Sent to FBI _____	____ Date Approving Authority ____ Date Approving Authority	☐ Cleared for Processing ☐ Request a Character Evaluation	____ Date Approving Authority ____ Date Approving Authority

The information on this form will be used in connection with an investigation of your character. Any information you wish to submit that you feel will expedite this investigation should be set forth.

CAUTION: Knowingly making a false statement on this form is a violation of Federal law and could result in criminal prosecution, significant civil penalties, and a denial of your loan. A false statement is punishable under 18 USC 1001 by imprisonment of not more than five years and/or a fine of not more than $10,000; under 15 USC 5 by imprisionment of not more than two years and/or a fine of not more than $5,000; and, if submitted by Federally insured institution, under 18 USC 1014 by prisionment of not more than twenty years and/or a fine of not more than $1,000,000.

Signature	Title	Date

against SBA's policy to provide assistance to persons not of good character and therefore consideration is given to the qualities and personality traits of a person, favorable and unfavorable relating thereto, ding behavior, integrity, candor and disposition toward criminal actions. It is also against SBA's policy to provide assistance not in the best interests of the United States, for example, if there is reason to ve that the effect of such assistance will be to encourage or support, directly or indirectly, activities inimical to the Security of the United States. Anyone concerned with the collection of this information, as to luntariness, disclosure of routine uses may contact the FOIA Office, 409 3rd St. S.W., and a copy of 9 "Agency Collection of Information" from SOP 40 04 will be provided.

SBA FORM 912 (12-93) SOP 9020 USE 5-87 EDITION UNTIL EXHAUSTED   TSoft Financial Software, Inc. © 1994 - 1995

se Note: The estimated burden hours for completion of this form is 15 minutes per response. If you have any questions or comments concerning this estimate or any other ct of this information collection please contact, Chief Administrative Information Branch, U.S. Small Business Administration 409 Third Street, S.W. Washington, D.C. 20416 or Waxman, Clearance Officer, Paperwork Reduction Project (3245-0178), Office of Management and Budget, Washington, D.C. 20503.

Illustration 3-K

SBA LOAN NUMBER

COMPENSATION AGREEMENT FOR SERVICES IN CONNECTION WITH APPLICATION AND LOAN FROM (OR IN PARTICIPATION WITH) SMALL BUSINESS ADMINISTRATION

The undersigned representative (attorney, accountant, engineer, appraiser, etc.) hereby agrees that the undersigned has not and will not, directly or indirectly, charge or receive any payment in connection with the application for or the making of the loan except for services actually performed on behalf of the Applicant. The undersigned futher agrees that the amount of payment for such services shall not exceed an amount deemed reasonable by SBA (and, if it is a participation loan, by the participating lending institution), and to refund any amount in excess of that deemed reasonable by SBA (and the participating institution). This agreement shall supersede any other agreement covering payment for such services.

A general description of the services performed, or to be performed, by the undersigned and the compensation paid or to be paid are set forth below. If the total compensation in any case exceeds $1,000 (or $300 for: (1) regular business loans of $15,000 or less; or (2) all disaster home loans) or if SBA should otherwise require, the services must be itemized on a schedule attached showing each date services were performed, time spent each day, and description of service rendered on each day listed.

The undersigned Applicant and representative hereby certify that no other fees have been charged or will be charged by the representative in connection with this loan, unless provided for in the loan authorization specifically approved by SBA.

GENERAL DESCRIPTION OF SERVICES

Paid Previously	$ _____ 0
Additional Amount to be Paid	$ _____ 0
Total Compensation	$ _____ 0

(Section 13 of the Small Business Act (15 USC 642) requires disclosures concerning fees. Parts 103, 108 and 120 of Title 13 of the Code of Federal Regulations contain provisions covering appearances and compensation of persons representing SBA applicants. Section 103.13-5 authorizes the suspension or revocation of the privilege of any such person to appear before SBA for charging a fee deemed unreasonable by SBA for services actually performed, charging of unreasonable expenses, or violation of this agreement. Whoever commits any fraud, by false or misleading statement or representation, or by conspiracy, shall be subject to the penalty of any applicable Federal or State statute.)

Dated _____ , 19 _____

(Representative)

By _____

The Applicant hereby certifies to the SBA that the above representations, description of services and amounts are correct and satisfactory to Applicant.

Dated _____ , 19 _____

(Applicant)

By _____

The participating lending institution hereby certifies that the above representations of service rendered and amounts charged are reasonable and satisfactory to it.

Dated _____ , 19 _____

(Lender)

By _____

NOTE: Foregoing certification must be executed, if by a corporation, in corporate name by duly authorized officer and duly attested; if by a partnership, in the firm name, together with the signature of a general partner.

SBA FORM 159 (2-93) REF SOP 70 50 Use 7-89 Edition Until Exhausted   TSoft Financial Software, Inc. © 1994 - 1995

Illustration 3-L

U.S. Small Business Administration

ASSURANCE OF COMPLIANCE FOR NONDISCRIMINATION

Applicant / Licensee/ Recipient / Subrecipient, (hereinafter referred to as applicant) in consideration of Federal financial assistance from the Small Business Administration, herewith agrees that it will comply with the nondiscrimination requirements of 13 CFR Parts 112 and 113 of the Regulations issued by the Small Business Administration (SBA).

13 CFR Parts 112, 113 and 117 require that no person shall on the grounds of age, color, handicap, marital status, national origin, race, religion or sex, be excluded from participation in, be denied the benefits of or otherwise be subjected to discrimination under any program or activity for which the applicant received Federal financial assistance from SBA.

Applicant agrees to comply with the recordkeeping requirements of 13 CFR 112.9, 113.5 and 117.9 as set forth in SBA Form 793, "Notice to New SBA Borrowers", to permit effective enforcement of 13 CFR 112, 113 and 117. Such recordkeeping requirements have been approved under OMB Number 3245-0076. Applicant further agrees to obtain or require similar Assurance of Compliance for Nondiscrimination from subrecipients, contractors/subcontractors, successors, transferees and assignees as long as it/they receive or retain possession of any Federal financial assistance from SBA. In the event the applicant fails to comply with any provision or requirement of 13 CFR Parts 112, 113 and 117. SBA may call, cancel, terminate, accelerate repayment or suspend any or all Federal financial assistance provided by SBA.

Executed the _____ day of _____ 19 _____

_____
Name, Address & Phone No. of Applicant

By _____
Typed Name & Title of Authorized Official

Corporate Seal

_____
Signature of Authorized Official

_____
Name, Address & Phone No. of Subrecipient

By _____
Typed Name & Title of Authorized Official

Corporate Seal

_____
Signature of Authorized Official

SBA FORM 652 (11-91) SOP 90 30
PREVIOUS EDITIONS OBSOLETE

TSoft Financial Software, Inc. © 1994 - 1995

Illustration 3-M

Certification Regarding
Debarment, Suspension, Ineligibility and Voluntary Exclusion
Lower Tier Covered Transactions

This certification is required by the regulations implementing Executive Order 12549 Debarment and Suspension, 13 CFR Part 145. The regulations were published as Part VII of the May 26, 1988 Federal Register (pages 19160-19211). Copies of the regulations may be obtained by contacting the person to which this proposal is submitted.

(BEFORE COMPLETING CERTIFICATION, READ INSTRUCTIONS ON REVERSE)

(1) The prospective lower tier participant certifies, by submission of this proposal, that neither it nor its principals are presently debarred, suspended, proposed for debarment, declared ineligible, or voluntarily excluded from participation in this transaction by any Federal department or agency.

(2) Where the prospective lower tier participant is unable to certify to any of the statements in this certification, such prospective participant shall attach an explanation to this proposal.

Business Name _____

Date _____   By _____
                                              Name and Title of Authorized Representative

                                         _____
                                         Signature of Authorized Representative

SBA Temporary Form 1624 (10-88)

• *Form 159 - Compensation Agreement* - This document is required to disclose to the SBA any professional fees which have been or will be paid by the borrower in connection with the SBA loan. This form is to be used for any consultants, accountants, attorneys, or other parties who have provided specific services or supporting documents to the borrower in preparing the SBA application or close the SBA loan. A copy of this form can be found on Illustration 3-K.

• *Form 652 - Assurance of Compliance for Nondiscrimination* - This document is required to attest that the borrower and any subsequent recipients of the SBA guaranteed loan proceeds agree to comply with SBA regulations pertaining to discrimination. These regulations require that no person be excluded from participation in, or be denied the benefits of any federal financial assistance from the SBA based on age, color, handicap, marital status, national origin, race, religion, or sex. A copy of this form can be found on Illustration 3-L.

• *Form 1624 - Certification Regarding Debarment* - This document is required to attest that the borrower, the individual, and the business entity have not been debarred from doing business with the federal government due to any administrative, disciplinary or other action specifically restricting the respective party. A copy of this form can be found on Illustration 3-M.

• *IRS Form 4506 - Request for Copy or Transcript of Tax Form* - This document permits the SBA to obtain a copy of the borrower's income tax return for verification comparison to the income tax returns submitted by the borrower in the loan application. A copy of this form can be found on Illustration 3-E.

• *Justification* - The lender (and therefore the borrower) has to provide justification for why the SBA guaranty should be provided for the proposed transaction. There is no regulation form on which to submit this information.

There are several reasons why SBA guaranteed loans are superior to conventional financing in the lending marketplace. These reasons include:

Terms - The SBA term limits allow the small business concern to borrow money for longer terms, which mean lower debt service and better cash flow for companies in their earlier years.

Interest Rates - In some instances, the interest rate caps on SBA guaranteed loans represent a lower rate than many small businesses would qualify for otherwise.

Qualification - Traditional lending sources avoid certain industries because of the inherent risks of lending money on special use assets, such as bowling allies or day care centers. The guaranty provides incentives for lenders to extend funds into these industries.

In addition, the SBA is sensitive to two particular uses of loan proceeds, both of which must be explained in order to justify the loan:

Change of Ownership - The lender must demonstrate that the borrower is purchasing an entity not as an investment, but rather as a business to be personally operated by the borrower. Further, the lender has to prove that the buyer and seller are not related, and that there is not better alternative financing available.

Refinancing Debt - The lender must demonstrate that there is a clear advantage to the borrower to refinance any debt with an SBA loan and that the previous loans have performed as agreed. The SBA will examine transcripts of the lender's previous loan to confirm that the lender is not unloading a bad loan on the agency.

There are a few additional SBA documents required with the loan application which must be prepared by the lender. These include Form 4-I (the Lender's Application for Guaranty) containing the Lender's Analysis, and Form 1846, the Statement Regarding Lobbying.

All documentation required by the lender to render a credit decision and to qualify for the SBA guaranty must be compiled by the lender and then submitted to the SBA. The lender must have approved the loan and be prepared to make it, subject to the SBA guaranty, before the SBA will review it.

While the list of data contained in this chapter may seem staggering, it is mostly information that is routinely available to and used by business owners.

Government regulations increase the size of this list annually - but this is not a problem which can be resolved or relaxed by the SBA and the lender.

The SBA and the lender have a responsibility to administer and abide by the law. To modify some of the more irrelevant, burdensome requirements of this process will require business owners to seek reform in Congress to alleviate some of the regulatory interference and costs of borrowing capital for small businesses.

Chapter 4

Explaining Circumstances

Some borrowers have faced special circumstances which weaken their loan application or dampen the lender's enthusiasm for considering their request. Because these situations require greater preparation, they can test the borrower's determination to get business financing.

These circumstances can vary, ranging from the indiscretions of youth to medical catastrophes. Often these circumstances have nothing to do with the borrower's past business performance, moral obligation to repay debts, or prospects for succeeding in the future. It is important for the borrower to be meticulously honest with the lender in discussing these situations. Was the borrower at fault? Was the borrower a victim? Can the borrower rehabilitate this financial condition?

The lender must evaluate if, based on this information, the borrower presents a greater risk and should therefore not be considered. This question is automatically answered affirmatively unless the borrower can convince the lender to investigate the previous problems in perspective.

The following suggestions are intended to assist borrowers in overcoming special conditions under which their personal credit record was tarnished through events beyond their control. These events need not prevent the borrower from advancing to the next opportunity in life. This discussion is not intended to instruct anyone how to develop excuses to perpetuate a record of failure, deceit or fraud. By following these important steps in explaining their situation, borrowers can develop thorough documentation to support explanations required in these matters.

Bankruptcy

Bankruptcy is a fact of life. Since bankruptcy protection statutes were liberalized in the 1980s, the number of businesses and individuals seeking protection has increased dramatically. From a business standpoint bankruptcy is often a legitimate strategy. It is a method to deal with overwhelming liabilities or a dire situation. Although sometime bankruptcy is abused, at times it can be the debtor's best logical decision.

But bankruptcy is not always a good strategy and can be very costly. Many businesses receive poor advice and seek bankruptcy prematurely without recognition of the consequences. Once that decision is made the debtor will live with it for many years.

Most loan officers have a knee - jerk reaction to parties who have sought protection under bankruptcy laws. In fact, many lenders treat bankruptcy as the ultimate violation of the borrower's morality. Legitimate bankruptcy cases do not involve morals - they are about money. Bankruptcy is usually not about an unwillingness to repay money, but rather the inability to repay money. Because most loan officers do not know much about bankruptcy, it is a challenge to obtain financing once it is part of the borrower's track record.

Bankruptcy cases are under the jurisdiction of a federal court to protect individuals or companies from their creditors in circumstances where the debtors liabilities exceed their assets. This protection is intended to prevent a particular creditor from unfairly collecting a debt at the expense of other creditors or beyond the debtor's realistic ability to pay. Bankruptcy can help debtors by providing time to reorganize their affairs in order to pay off debts without undue interference from creditors.

There are three basic classes of bankruptcy:

Chapter 7 - This class of bankruptcy is for liquidation of the debtor's estate to settle claims against it. The proceeds are distributed against claims which are prioritized by the court.

Chapter 11- This class of bankruptcy is for the reorganization of businesses (or high net worth individuals) in which debtors are permitted to restructure their financial affairs in order to pay their debts.

Chapter 13 - This class of bankruptcy is for individuals (with assets less than $350,000) to restructure or renegotiate the repayment terms of their liabilities with creditors. Regular payments are made through a court-appointed trustee until all debts are repaid.

There are countless circumstances which lead parties to seek the protection of a bankruptcy court. Without doubt, many parties are forced to choose this strategy due to events beyond their control. In some cases borrowers will have the chance to overcome the stigma of bankruptcy and to obtain new financing for starting over. Chances are better if the bankruptcy was an individual case rather than a business case.

Consider three true-life examples of justifiable bankruptcies:

The first example involved a mother who delivered a premature baby. In receiving the best available medical treatment, the baby stayed in the hospital for six months. Thirty days after the child was released from the hospital, the parents were expected to pay a $300,000 invoice.

During the pregnancy term the father was laid off from an international airline that had filed for bankruptcy protection. The airline abruptly (and illegally) stopped paying medical insurance premiums for its employees. With neither insurance coverage nor a job, the father could not produce $300,000 on short notice.

Filing bankruptcy was the only way for this family to protect itself from claims made by the hospital and doctors. It was not indicative of how well these people had previously managed their financial affairs, nor should it have cast hard working, productive people into financial purgatory.

How could they recreate a positive financial record without additional credit being extended to them? Fortunately an understanding lender listened, worked a little harder, and provided financing for a new business that put this family on the way to rebuilding their lives.

A second example involved an ambitious chiropractor who started his own practice six weeks after graduation without a sufficient number of patients. After obtaining a high interest loan and easy credit to buy start-up equipment, he did not have enough patients to earn money for the payments.

Bankruptcy was the only way that one creditor was stopped from literally walking off with the doctor's medical equipment during the treatment of a patient. Should the misjudgment of an aggressive young doctor be a lifelong impediment to moving on to financial success?

While employed by another clinic for four years, this doctor got his affairs in order. He then secured a loan to finance the purchase and improvement of a building to house his own growing practice. He now employs eight people and pays a lot of taxes because a practical lender listened and responded to his loan application.

The third example is one of the most famous corporate bankruptcy cases involved a publicly owned company known as Manville Corporation. This manufacturing company had a comfortable position in the marketplace selling a variety of building materials.

One of their most successful products was an asbestos-based insulation material. For many years the company sold millions of dollars worth of this asbestos insulation. When asbestos was later determined to be a carcinogen, Manville discontinued use of this material.

This information led to a flood of lawsuits against the company from thousands of persons who had come into contact with this insulation and later developed cancer. Manville was faced with a catastrophic liability that would have continued to grow until it consumed the company. Protection in bankruptcy court enabled the company to manage these undefined liabilities while continuing to operate. This action insured its ability to survive and pay all eventual claims which were filed.

This strategy was a bold move which changed how bankruptcy is viewed. Using bankruptcy as an offensive strategy permitted the company to settle its liabilities, which would have never been accomplished without court protection.

Obviously bankruptcy can be abused, but recognition must be given to its legitimate use in circumstances which threaten individuals and businesses. Some lenders are shortsighted to adjudge that parties seeking bankruptcy protection do not have adequate moral standards. Each case must be evaluated according to its own particular circumstances.

The loan officer cannot assume that borrowers have a character flaw due to their involvement in a bankruptcy case. There are many cases where overzealous or unreasonable creditors have forced bankruptcies rather than seeking more prudent remedies to deal with problem loans. Lenders must recognize that another lender's inflexibility can lead to mistakes which cause some borrowers to be unjustly penalized.

Lenders must consider the circumstances surrounding any borrower who has been involved in a bankruptcy case. Sometimes a better test of character is watching how the borrower manages to emerge after a bankruptcy case.

Borrowers involved in a previous bankruptcy may actually be a lower risk for lenders. These borrowers have a wealth of experience in dealing with difficult situations, better preparing them for the economic risks associated with operating a small business. Surviving these tough circumstances adds to the borrower's management and financial education.

Federal bankruptcy statutes restrict how soon individuals with previous involvement in a bankruptcy case can access protection again. This limitation protects subsequent lenders who deal with these borrowers.

If the borrower has been involved in a bankruptcy case (personal or business), the lender will discover this fact very early in the application process. It is better to disclose the facts before the lender reads this information in a credit report.

Before referring to the bankruptcy, borrowers should have the loan officer interested in the transaction. If the loan officer is not comfortable with the attributes of the deal before learning about the bankruptcy, the borrower will never get the lender's full attention on the application.

Credit reports include information about prior connections with any bankruptcy. In addition to personal bankruptcy cases, the credit report records any business in which the borrower was an owner, shareholder, or partner. Even if borrowers have no control over the events leading to a business bankruptcy, they must be prepared to explain the circumstances of the case.

Because the proceedings of a bankruptcy case are a matter of public record, the lender is able to obtain a copy of the borrower's case file to verify the dates, creditors, debts, and final results of the case. In other words, a borrower's fictional account of the bankruptcy case could permanently destroy credibility with the lender.

In addition to telling the loan officer the bankruptcy story, the borrower should provide a written version for review purposes. Because the loan officer will probably have to relay the information in writing, it is better for the borrower to transcribe a detailed account as the basis for the lender's report.

The borrower should document the circumstances thoroughly and substantiate any difficulties which led to seeking bankruptcy protection. If debtors were not at fault, they should prove it by using affidavits from other parties, accident reports, medical records, pictures, newspaper articles, and any other information available to support these claims.

Former bankrupt debtors should prepare a detailed summary of how the case was resolved and what they did after the case was dismissed. This brief needs to be supported with documents verifying the borrower's personal involvement in the situation, court filings, financial reports, and trustee's report. How the borrower's affairs have changed since the bankruptcy? What has been accomplished to put the borrower's financial affairs in order?

If the bankruptcy experience was due to imprudent management rather than tragic circumstances, the truth is equally as important. Depending on how much time has lapsed, how much money was lost by the creditors, and how the borrower has managed in the post-petition period, the lender may still consider the loan application.

Litigation

Living in the most litigious society in the world can give a new meaning to the term liability. Because over 75% of the world's lawyers are in the United States, American citizens have higher odds of being sued over a dispute. This exposure is increased for small business owners. People can spend considerable sums defending themselves and can damage their financial condition merely by being accused.

When the borrower's financial statement is scarred with the extraordinary costs of defending a suit, or when the borrower has settled a suit to limit these costs, the loan officer is entitled to a detailed explanation. By putting the matter in context and perspective, the loan officer can understand the impact of the litigation the company's finances. This explanation helps the borrower move the application process beyond the legal situation allowing the positive aspects of the loan proposal to be considered and emphasized.

The lender should receive copies of the lawsuit and the borrower's answer. In justifying the defensive side of the dispute, the borrower can provide the lender with copies of invoices, receipts, and other documents to show how the business was affected. If the borrower's attorney has detailed a favorable opinion of the borrower's situation, the lender should be given copies of this correspondence.

At least the loan officer will understand the borrower's situation after this disclosure and not fear the risk of unknown parameters. But even if sympathetic, the loan officer retains the responsibility of underwriting the loan request. The loan officer will have to take the result of the litigation on the business into account, regardless of whether or not the borrower was at fault.

Most lenders will not proceed with a loan request if there is a material lawsuit pending at the time of the application. Routine matters which occur in the normal course of business, and which do not threaten the borrower's financial condition, should not interfere with the loan application. But if there is a matter of any substance against the company which is unresolved or on appeal, the lender will probably wait until final judgment has been rendered before proceeding.

Any judgment against the borrower could significantly change the financial condition. If the borrower were forced into a large settlement, or if the other party were enabled to lien the borrower's assets, the lender could suddenly have a problem loan. The collateral assets securing the loan could possibly have more claims outstanding than value.

If the situation has already cleared the judicial process and the borrower is faced with a judgment, the lender will be interested in how the matter is handled. If the borrower loses in court, the judgment must be honored. The lender will be interested in how the borrower reacts because it may be indicative of the borrower's response would react in a similar dispute with the lender at some future date.

Divorce

The number of divorces being filed today is staggering and can be disastrous for a small business owner. Because the process can be strenuous for the individuals involved, they may have months of under-performance in their business responsibilities. In addition, the financial settlement can be very disruptive if the borrower is forced to buy out or share the business ownership interests with the other spouse.

If the business owner has recently completed the divorce process, it is important to provide an explanation to the lender about any impact the divorce had on the business or the owner's personal financial condition. The borrower should document this explanation with copies of bank records, financial statements, and a copy of the final divorce settlement. Disclosing personal (that is, emotional rather than financial) aspects of the divorce should be omitted, not only as irrelevant, but also as potentially detrimental to the loan application.

Because of the stressful issues in divorce cases, the vengeful actions of one party may create liabilities for the other party. Alternatively, one party may refuse to pay legitimately allocated liabilities which are in the joint names of both parties. Divorce can become a disaster to the borrower's credit history and ability to borrower money.

These circumstances need to be carefully documented in order to demonstrate the borrower's innocence in such a situation. Divorce is probably the most abused excuse used by persons with bad credit. To earn credibility the borrower has to show how the bad credit was created through the irresponsible actions of others.

The best defense is to pay off any unpaid accounts whether individually or jointly held. The borrower should try to protect a good credit history when possible, later pursuing the other party for recovery of these sums. To limit exposure, the borrower should close the joint credit accounts when the divorce process first begins and notify creditors that the borrower will not be responsible for future liabilities created on a joint account. While the borrower cannot escape joint and several liability on existing balances, a notice can prevent a creditor from holding the borrower liable for subsequent charges.

After discovering negative credit report information as a result of the divorce, the borrower should contact the credit bureau and provide a statement detailing the situation. The credit bureau is obligated to include this explanation in all future inquiries.

If the divorce is not yet finalized, the borrower should consider waiting until the process is over before making a business loan application. When the owner is resolving the emotional and complicated issues of divorce, the anxiety of seeking credit is compounded. The borrower benefits by focusing on the business at hand - one major negotiation at a time.

Bad Decisions

To err is human, but some mistakes are more costly than others. In a dynamic economy, strategic decisions must be made on a regular basis. Because small business owners are constantly making decisions with long term implications, errors will sometimes be made.

In a changing world small business owners often perform as the chief executive officer, chief financial officer, chief operating officer, advertising agent, transportation specialist, tax expert, and computer prodigy; then they go home to be a compassionate parent, loving spouse, and supportive partner! These roles are defined by a constant stream of ideas from newspapers, magazines, cable features, sitcoms, talk shows, books, videos, MTV, C-SPAN, pay-per-view, e-mail, and the internet. So how can anyone make mistakes?

We live in an age overrun with ideas and communication. Today's eighth wonder-of-the-world is tomorrow's Cro Magnum mummy. More decisions are demanded than ever before but we are still limited to one brain.

This explanation is given in order to offer universal forgiveness for making occasional bad business decisions. As long as the decision is based on the best option at the time, it should not be reconsidered. When the borrower documents an error for the lender, this page should be submitted with the loan request to provide some perspective to the loan officer.

When the loan officer is told about errors, the borrower's candor is factored into an assessment of the actions taken to overcome the mistake. If the borrower qualifies under the other criteria necessary to obtain financing, previous errors should not prevent the borrower from getting a loan.

Bad Health

Consider what would happen to the economic status of a borrower who becomes ill for an extended period. There are many possible consequences and most of them include serious financial damage. Should that mean that the borrower can never qualify for business credit? What if the borrower had a spotless track record before the illness? It hardly seems fair that after battling a disease to save one's life the borrower would also have to battle for the survival of the business. Once the borrower's health recovers, there is hard work for the business to recover.

The answer is to provide documentation to communicate and confirm the medical situation to the lender. The loan officer wants to know how the illness affected the borrower personally and how that impacted the operation of the business. Borrowers can expect compassion for these situations but should accept the burden of proof. Rather than telling the loan officer all of the details of the medical treatment and procedures, a generic description of the medical condition will provide enough personal information. Because borrowers want the lender interested in their economic health, the discussion should focus on the financial details.

Bad Credit

Compounding several of the problems mentioned above is the trickle-down effect each has on the borrower's personal credit history. If the borrower's cash flow is interrupted for any reason and cash reserves are exhausted, payments to creditors will slow down accordingly. This problem must eventually be dealt with, since slow credit payments are one of the most troublesome problems in the eyes of the lender.

It is important to manage personal credit closely to keep one's payment history clean and avoid perpetuating negative entries into a credit record. Lenders focus on a number of aspects in the credit report, including the total amount of credit outstanding, payment history, and any public records which indicate the unsatisfactory conduct of personal affairs.

Understanding how to manage this process cannot repair one's previous poor credit record. But modifying current and future performance can improve a borrower's situation and end the poor performance reflected in the recent credit report. Borrowers should begin by using the following strategies:

- Payoff as much credit as possible by using savings, having a yard sale, taking back recently purchased merchandise, liquidating assets, borrowing money from the business, collecting outstanding debts, or even drawing down the cash surrender value of a life insurance policy. Cash should be obtained (without borrowing more) to pay off these accounts as fast as possible. Rather than reducing all the accounts, the ones with the lower balances should be paid off. It is better to have five past due accounts than ten past due accounts.

- After the small debts are cleared, borrowers should prioritize by paying off debt with higher payments or higher interest rates first. Paying off these accounts first gives the borrower more flexibility in the future.

- Payments should be managed so as not to go beyond thirty days past due if possible, even if it means hand-delivering the payment. Payments less than thirty days late are not reported to the credit bureau.

- If cash shortage is temporary, the borrower should arrange to limit the number of creditors who will receive late payments. Rather than making one $500 payment on time and being late on four payments of $125, it is better to pay the four accounts on time and be late only on the one $500 payment.

- The credit bureau does not receive reports of late payments from such liabilities as public utilities, telephone companies, long distance suppliers, cable operators, merchandise buying clubs, and private note holders. Slowing payments to these accounts will not affect a public credit record and may help keep it clean. Getting too far behind on utility bills, however, will risk disconnection of that service requiring a deposit to be paid to restore service.

128

If the borrower has bad credit, the lender should be told why. Often bad credit is not the result of poor management or lack of responsibility, but rather circumstances which affect the borrower's ability to meet those responsibilities consistently. To earn the lender's confidence, the borrower must demonstrate that those circumstances have been improved to a degree which will not interfere with the borrower's ability to make payments on the loan being requested.

Chapter 5

Improving the Odds of Loan Approval

Complete and Organized Information

The easiest strategy to get a loan proposal approved is to provide the loan officer with the necessary information in an organized manner. Too many borrowers are needlessly rejected or delayed because they do not take the time to provide adequate documentation.

The lender has to completely understand the borrower's operation (its history and future) and the loan request. All of this information should be documented in order to provide a complete picture of the business including the facts and figures necessary to approve the proposed loan. Without sufficient data to answer all of the questions, the loan officer will either have to ask for more information or take the easy way out by saying "no" to the proposal.

Often the borrower will have the loan officer's complete attention at the first meeting when the loan proposal is submitted. The loan officer may be ready to get started on the request immediately after this meeting. If the process is delayed by the borrower's failure to provide sufficient information or promptly respond to the loan officer's inquiries, the loan officer may lose any momentum created for the deal.

The borrower should be on the offensive with information and answers about the business while the loan officer is interested and attentive to the loan proposal. Stretching the process out over weeks, which can easily become months, makes the loan more difficult to approve. The lender will either lose focus on it or will be less enthusiastic about assisting the borrower.

Anticipating what data will be needed and which questions will be asked should not be difficult for an experienced person in business. Preparing this information in advance will make a positive impression about the borrower's management capabilities and competence.

Based on the information listed in Chapter Three, the borrower should assemble any data which might possibly be relevant to the loan request. By providing information in the initial meeting, the borrower increases the lender's responsibility to respond without delayed consideration. Because each borrower's situation is unique, it is impossible to anticipate every item the lender will need to evaluate the loan request. But the borrower should be prepared to respond quickly and thoroughly.

Positive Thinking

However strong or weak the borrower's proposal is, it will sound better if presented in a confident, enthusiastic tone. The positive demeanor of the borrower can be effective in gaining the loan officer's favorable impression of the proposal. Enthusiasm is important to demonstrate that the borrower is confident about the purpose and goals of the business. This confidence will carry over into the loan officer's review, assisting the lender in approving the transaction.

By accentuating the positive, the borrower concentrates on the successes and not on the failures. Even if the business has suffered its share of losses, the emphasis should be on the wins - the upbeat stories which reinforce the reasons for lending money to this company.

The Only Way to Get an Answer is to Ask

Business people often hear horror stories from other small businesses about the condition of the lending market. Innuendoes, rumors, and negative tales convince many borrowers that there are no funds available. But what the borrower hears is only one side of the story. Just because someone else gets turned down for a loan does not mean the time is bad to apply for a loan. As described throughout this book, there are many parameters on which a loan request is judged, any one of which can justify a lender to deny someone's request for financing.

The borrower should concentrate on getting the loan approved on its merits, without being discouraged by the failure of others. Even if there are flaws which will concern the lender, the worst thing that can happen is that the loan officer will say "no." If the borrower does not ask, the loan officer cannot say "yes."

Convincing the lender to provide financing is much like selling the borrower's services or products. The borrower has to identify prospects, qualify them, make the pitch, and close the deal. Getting the lender to make a loan requires the same steps.

After researching the market, the borrower can determine which lenders are prospects to handle the transaction. Which lender is best suited to provide the services to the borrower? Which lender is interested in the market in which this business is conducted. Which lender wants the borrower's business? Which lender is willing to invest the time, confidence, and funding to help the borrower succeed?

Does this lender understand the borrower's business? Is the lender interested in what the borrower is trying to accomplish? Does the lender feel comfortable with small businesses at the borrower's stage of growth? Is the lender qualified and experienced in lending with the SBA loan guaranty program? Can the lender feel comfortable with the borrower's strategy? Does the lender recognize how the borrower addresses the risks involved?

If the lender passes these qualifications, the borrower should lay out the proposal and ask for the loan. Presenting the loan request confidently, the borrower should have an organized, complete package of information - concise, clearly stated, convincing, and supported by the borrower's assumptions.

In addition, the borrower should prepare for the loan officer's objections. Questions need to be answered with direct, documented information which

132

satisfies the loan officer's concern. Rather than assuming that the reply is sufficient, the borrower should ask the loan officer if the question has been fully answered.

It is easier to answer a question before it is asked. By anticipating questions, the answers can be included in the loan application. In that manner, the borrower benefits by controlling the slant and specifics of the information.

If the borrower is not sure how to answer a specific question, it is best to call the loan officer back as soon as practical to provide the response. The phone call should be followed with a letter to reiterate the answer.

In concluding the meeting, the borrower should summarize the business strategy, restate the deal, and review the answered objections. The goal is to make it easy and logical for the loan officer and the lender to give a positive reply to the loan request.

Dealing Directly With Negative Information

If part of the borrower's history includes a horror tale, such as one of the situations described in Chapter Four, it should not be hidden. As suggested in other sections of the book, the borrower should make sure the lender is interested in the positive attributes of the proposition before venturing into life's tragedies. But after becoming serious about the proposal, the loan officer should be led gently through the negative part of the story of the special circumstances.

In Chapter Four there are suggestions about how to discuss several sensitive situations which the borrower may have experienced. By not apologizing for these events, the borrower acknowledges that they are an integral part to past experiences. It is unlikely that the borrower purposely intended to encounter some of these situations.

The lender is not likely to be particularly sympathetic or concerned. The borrower should not care if the lender is forgiving. What the borrower needs is the lender's open-minded recognition that these past events do not preclude the borrower's future events and that they will not preclude the borrower getting a business loan.

Understanding the lender's perspective of these circumstances will help the borrower predict the reaction and will therefore help the borrower prepare for this disclosure. The key objectives are to not alarm the lender and to provide assurances that the borrower does not have a character flaw, has a bright future, and represents an acceptable business risk.

Documentation about the event is important. How have these events affected the borrower? How has the borrower tried to minimize these effects for the benefit of family and creditors (in that order of importance)? What has transpired since the event and how has the borrower diligently and capably recovered? Honesty is the best policy, even if it hurts. The more direct the information from the borrower, the better equipped the borrower is to get another chance.

Meeting at the Borrower's Office

As simple as it sounds, meeting on the borrower's turf can provide an advantage when presenting a loan proposal. When loan officers are away from their desks, they are more vulnerable to listening to borrowers without the defenses normally provided to them when the borrowers are in their office.

The loan officer cannot be distracted or interrupted in the borrower's offices. There are no phone calls, letters to sign, or memos of review. Meeting at the borrower's place of business makes any additional information the loan officer may request accessible, and permits the loan officer to view the borrower's management and leadership first hand.

The most important advantage is that the loan officer can see, hear, smell and touch the borrower's business: customers, the store, busy employees, and the loading docks accepting and shipping inventory. Because the level of activity (if relevant) can also have a positive effect on the loan officer, the lender's visit should be scheduled during busier hours when there are a lot of customers, employees, machines, or other movement involved. Translating the vision of the operation from the loan proposal to other people will be easier if the loan officer can describe it from this first-person recollection.

Not Enough Collateral?

Most denied loan proposals are due to insufficient collateral. Borrowers cannot always reduce the amount of funds needed, and the lender is usually not able or willing to extend beyond the normal collateral coverage requirements. Sometimes there are minor ways to enhance or stretch the values of collateral assets to provide the lender with sufficient coverage, or at least to get the borrower close enough to convince the lender to give consideration.

Examining the lender's valuation method - The borrower should make sure the lender is using accurate, reliable information when determining the value of the borrower's collateral. This suggestion may require the borrower to invest in a second opinion with another appraiser. If that second opinion convinces the lender to increase the loan, it is worth the time and cost.

If the collateral includes real estate, the borrower should be aware that increased scrutiny of real estate lending in the past several years has resulted in a myriad of new regulations and requirements of appraisers. The effect of these changes has been a general depression of real estate valuations, due to the appraisal industry's fear of future challenges of its assessments.

An appraisal is an estimate of value, based on three distinct valuation approaches: market, replacement cost, and income approach. Most full appraisals assess a valuation using each of the three approaches to determine a final statement of value based on a weighted average of the three, depending on the specifics of the property. In general terms, the three approaches are defined as follows:

> • *Market value* - This approach measures the likely value of a property based on recent, comparable sales ("comps") of similar properties in the general area. The appraiser attempts to find other nearby sales of properties of the same size and scale of improvement.

> • *Replacement Cost* - This approach measures the likely cost of rebuilding the improvements on a particular property, plus the current value of the land based on comparable sales.

> • *Income Approach* - When applicable, the appraiser examines the income being generated by a property, or the likely income generated from similar properties in the same area, based on prevailing market rents.

The borrower should be aware that appraisers have varying degrees of familiarity with the immediate geographic area and the type of improvement the borrower owns. The borrower should cooperate fully with the appraiser when the property is examined. It is a good idea to be on hand and to be prepared to provide any information the appraiser requests. The more information the appraiser has, the more accurate valuation the borrower will receive.

If the collateral includes furniture, fixtures, and equipment (FF&E), the borrower should examine the method under which the lender values this collateral. Most lenders will routinely discount these assets 50%, but the borrower should notice whether that valuation is based on the book value or the cost value. The borrower should encourage the loan officer to use the cost of the asset, since depreciation on most of these assets do not really affect their liquidation value.

If the FF&E is a major portion of the collateral assets, the borrower may even decide to request an appraisal. In doing so, risks can be reduced if the borrower carefully guides the lender to a capable appraiser.

Too often, lenders use liquidation companies and auctioneers for appraisals of FF&E assets. The liquidation value is based on liquidation-type sales and is therefore going to be substantially less than the true value of the asset. Liquidation value assumes that the asset is sold on a distressed basis. If sold over a reasonable time period, the asset would carry a much higher value.

Many lenders have a knee-jerk reaction to collateral liquidation, due to an unpleasant past experience. The borrower has to counteract that attitude with assurance about how the lender could reasonably expect to recover the loan when collateral is liquidated correctly. Lenders are apt to want to liquidate the collateral too fast, which depresses sale prices.

It's no secret that buyers see blood when they watch a nervous loan officer pacing around an equipment auction, wondering how much of a loss is going to be taken. A better sale method would be to place the FF&E on consignment with a used equipment or furniture dealer, letting them sell the assets over a reasonable time frame when market demand will pay a higher price. These are the same dealers who are only too glad to buy the FF&E for ten cents on the dollar at the lender's auction.

The borrower should know the value of the assets on a liquidation basis, after understanding how to liquidate those assets on a reasonable basis. This information will permit the borrower to negotiate stronger collateral valuations with the loan officer, and insure that the loan officer gives the borrower adequate credit for the collateral assets.

Offering the lender other assets - If collateral assets are short, the borrower can offer to pledge other assets to the lender so that the loan will meet the lender's requirements. Other assets can sometimes cover a small margin needed by the lender as an alternative to lowering the loan amount.

When using this methodology, the borrower should be prepared to be generous in supplying whatever is available. If loan officers do not ask for a particular asset in the beginning, then they probably do not place much value on it.

These other assets may have marginal value, but if totaled, could provide the lender with a substantial contribution toward eliminating any collateral shortfall which may exist. These assets may include the borrower's FF&E, automobiles, rolling stock, accounts receivable, inventory, cash surrender value of insurance policies, notes receivable, and other miscellaneous assets on the borrower's business or personal balance sheet.

Maximizing the valuation of current assets - Small business lenders usually do not attach much value to the accounts receivable and inventory assets of a borrower. This failure to recognize value of these assets is prudent, since both can disappear in days unless the lender could control them.

Borrowers are often frustrated at the difficulty to leverage current asset strength, unless they are is willing to pay 25% to 30% for factored loans from asset-based lenders. The margin of adequate financing is sometimes tied up in the current assets of a business, seemingly untouchable at a reasonable cost to the borrower.

One method to increase the leverage of these current assets is to request the loan officer to include them in the borrower's collateral pool as contribution toward the collateral requirements of the borrower's term loan. The borrower can enhance the value to these assets by offering to permit the lender to monitor the assets and by being willing to pay related service fees to the lender for the cost of such monitoring.

In other words, if the lender would give the borrower credit for a lower-than-average advance percentage on current assets (for example, a 50% advance on 60-day receivables and a 35% advance on inventory), this credit would provide the borrower with the margin of collateral needed to get the loan proposal approved. In exchange for the lender approving a long-term loan with short-term collateral, the borrower would allow the lender to monitor these assets to insure adequate coverage continues.

The borrower would be required to provide the lender with a regular statement of asset values, on perhaps a weekly or monthly basis. This statement would detail the changes of accounts receivable and inventory, along with defining the components that comprise these asset totals. The borrower would also have to be willing to pay the lender the extra cost of reviewing these statements each period, recognizing the legitimate effort required over the term of the loan. These fees may equate to 1% to 2% of the loan balance each year.

This option is infrequently employed and is suited only for established businesses with a long track record of successful operations and good management systems. As a creative option, it may make the difference in qualifying for a loan. After the loan has been serviced for a couple of years, and the principal balance has been paid down below the normal margin required of the main collateral assets, the borrower may negotiate a release of the current asset collateral in order to lower costs and reporting requirements.

The Rope Theory - Projecting Performance

Borrowers are always required to provide the loan officer with projections of the company's financial performance for at least two years. These estimates are intended to give the loan officer confidence that the borrower can service the debt with cash flow from operations.

These projections are more difficult to estimate for start-up businesses or for businesses intending to use the loan proceeds for making major changes in their operations. It is incumbent on the borrower to use caution and salesmanship when developing these projections, since these numbers are a very important component to ultimate loan approval.

Financial projections can be described as a "Rope Theory." The borrower has the opportunity to *swing* or *hang*, depending on the success and accuracy of the projections.

The borrower can *swing* by using the projections persuasively, convincing the loan officer that the loan proceeds will enable the borrower either to increase profitable revenues or reduce specific costs in order to provide the monies to make future loan payments. The *rope* enables the borrower to obtain the funds needed to accomplish this success.

138

But if the projections do not come to fruition, then the borrower will *hang*. Loan default is certain, caused by an inadequate cash flow available to service the debt. This situation will lead to liquidation of the collateral assets, as well as a possible lawsuit against the borrower and any loan guarantors.

Any persuasive presentation to promote the borrower's ability to perform has to be reinforced with actual performance. In this sense, financial projections can be a powerful tool for the borrower to use in convincing the loan officer of the prudence of the proposed loan. But these same projections can smother the borrower with an untenable situation which could lead to the company's demise.

Companion Loans

Most lenders and borrowers have approached the legal limitations of the SBA guaranty as an actual limitation on the loan size of an SBA guaranteed loan. This limitation does not exist, however, and the perceptions of it has prevented many businesses and lenders from negotiating many good loans.

The regulations provide for loan guaranty limits, based on the term and size of the loan. These regulations determine that the guaranty not exceed a particular percentage of the loan (for example, 75% or 80%), but they do not require the guaranty to equate to that level. That is, the regulations which permit the lender to extend a 75% guaranteed loan do not prevent the lender from extending a 65% or 45% guaranteed loan.

Often lenders will set an artificial maximum loan limit for borrowers in order to achieve the maximum SBA guaranty on each loan. But if the borrower has the financial capacity and an eligible need for a higher loan amount, there is no SBA restriction on the lender's ability to make a larger loan. Characteristic of their conservative nature, some lenders are merely hesitant to fall below the maximum guaranteed leverage limit.

One method employed by many lenders to make larger guaranteed loans without taking on more exposure, has been the use of a senior companion loan. For example, a borrower may want $1,300,000 to finance the purchase of a motel. Many SBA lenders would limit their offer to a $1,000,000 loan since this loan would carry the maximum SBA guaranty of 75% or $750,000.

However, a more creative lender could actually make a $300,000 first mortgage loan with a $1,000,000 second mortgage loan backed with the SBA guaranty. The lender's senior loan is not guaranteed, but is effectively protected by the subordinated SBA loan, which allows the lender to protect the senior financing in case of a liquidation scenario.

This companion loan method enables the marketplace to bridge the gap between regulatory restrictions and the true needs of the borrowing business sector. These situations highlight the fact that Congress has not updated the limitations on SBA guaranteed loans to meet the realities faced by small businesses.

Start-Up Businesses

Regardless of the borrower's industry or business, the toughest loan for a lender to consider is to a start-up business. In almost all circumstances, this phase of a business is the most difficult for the borrower, and certainly the most risky for the lender.

In focusing on the risks faced by the lender in this situation, the borrower needs to overcome the skepticism which accompanies the loan officer's desire to help. The loan officer has to be assured that the borrower effectively can marshal available resources to generate profitable revenues quickly enough to survive and repay the loan as scheduled. For a start-up business loan, there is greater emphasis on equity capital, because the lender wants the borrower to have enough cash reserve to meet unexpected expenses or unanticipated slowness in sales.

If the borrower is a start-up business, the following items required in the loan application (discussed in Chapter Three) need special emphasis to overcome the lender's aversion to this stage of business lending:

Borrower's Equity - The lender will be adamant about requiring a strong capital contribution from the borrower in the form of operating cash. There is no substitute for operating funds to insure that the borrower can weather the start-up phase of the business, which always produces many unforeseen expenses.

The borrower's revenue expectations, if over or under estimated, can also play havoc with the cash requirements of the start-up period. The borrower should have a readily available source of short-term working capital to manage these requirements in the likely event that the financial projections are inaccurate.

Financial Projections - The borrower's financial projections are going to be scrutinized very carefully, because start-up borrowers do not have a previous track record against which to compare the reasonableness of these numbers. Every figure will be questioned when the projections are presented to the lender.

Income and expense projections should be constructed realistically. The borrower cannot perform too much research on these figures. What kind of marketing efforts are required to produce sales? What fixed expenses are involved in opening the business? What variable costs are incurred at the level of sales projected?

Borrowers should consult with non-competitors in similar markets to determine whether or not the projections are attainable. Experienced business owners who will not be affected can quickly evaluate the forecasts to insure that the borrower has not missed something significant which could lead to disaster.

Feasibility - The borrower should make an effort to demonstrate to the lender that the new business idea is feasible and that the borrower can, in fact, succeed with the plan. In identifying the demand for the product or service, the borrower must show the experience or ability to meet that demand.

The country is littered with the skeletons of great business ideas that were not thought out far enough. One former professional football player started a local chain of necktie stores to capitalize on his popularity and the attention his stylish and colorful neckties had received. Unfortunately, he lived in Miami, Florida where much of the local business community does not wear neckties frequently because of the tropical climate.

Marketing Plan - Borrowers must demonstrate to the lender that they have identified the target audience and have ascertained the most effective method of attracting that audience to the business. Good businesses must have lots of paying customers to become great businesses.

Borrowers should consult with advertising consultants who not only place advertising, but who develop ideas for communicating to the consumer group most likely to buy the borrower's products or services. Most start-up businesses do not have enough money to determine marketing through trial and error.

If the borrower is a franchised company, much of this function will be purchased as part of the package. In addition, it is wise to consult with a specialist in the market area to test the franchiser's assumptions about how to advertise the business locally.

Start-up businesses should expect to have a more difficult job getting a loan approved. But emphasis on these items will assist in giving the loan officer confidence in the most important factors of the business: cash flow and revenue generation.

Chapter 6

Getting the Loan Closed

Now What Happens?

Once the loan has been approved by the lender and the SBA, the lender is responsible for setting the activities in motion to have the loan transaction executed (commonly referred to as "closed") and funded. This process is somewhat involved in itself, despite all of the work that has be expended getting the application assembled and the loan approved.

The loan closing phase requires the borrower to produce additional documentation specific to the collateral assets. The lender's attorney is charged with preparing the loan and security documents according to the SBA Loan Authorization and Agreement and with insuring that all parties are in compliance with the terms described therein. The lender may or may not take an active role in the process.

Borrowers frequently get frustrated at the time required to move from SBA approval to actually funding the loan. It is typically not until this stage that the myriad of professional assistants become involved: appraisers, engineers, surveyors, and attorneys. The borrower is usually hesitant to spend money on the required due diligence required before having the loan formally approved. There is much work to be done, and, usually the borrower is in line with several other borrowers for the services which are needed.

The first activity required is for the lender and lender's attorney to review the SBA Loan Authorization and Agreement, insuring that it accurately reflects the lender's understanding of and intent for the transaction. If not, changes have to be addressed with the SBA in writing, which may or may not delay further closing activity. Once the lender has confirmed this information, the parties are ready to start working toward a closing.

Next, the lender or closing attorney will engage in a series of activities for which the borrower will be obligated to pay - whether or not the loan is ever closed. Depending on the borrower's collateral, the lender will order a title and lien search, an appraisal, an environmental report, and a survey. The results of these reports are needed to confirm the assumptions the lender is depending on to go forward with the loan.

Should any of these reports come back with different results than expected, or with newly identified problems, there may be additional time delays, a modification of the loan terms, or even withdrawal of the lender's commitment. It is important for the borrower to understand the dynamics of this stage of the closing, to insure that the lender does not overreact to unexpected results. This information is discussed further in this chapter.

The borrower should remember that the closing attorney is not an arbitrary participant in the closing process. The closing attorney represents only the lender. One attorney cannot represent two parties in the same transaction. Whether the borrower should be represented by an attorney is a different question and is addressed in Chapter Seven.

This chapter will discuss the activities which are common for loan closings, why these activities are needed, and what the associated costs are likely to be. Further, this chapter describes ways the borrower can shorten the time necessary to get the loan closed and maybe even reduce some of the associated costs.

The SBA Authorization and Loan Agreement

The first step toward closing the loan is when the lender obtains the SBA Authorization and Loan Agreement ("Authorization") from the SBA. This document contains the terms and conditions under which the SBA will provide the loan guaranty to the lender. The lender must comply with the provisions of this document to the letter or risk having the SBA guaranty canceled.

Typically fourteen to sixteen pages in length, the Authorization describes the loan transaction, its term, the required collateral, the guarantors, and the other negotiated conditions. The lender's attorney uses the Authorization to develop the specific set of closing documents needed to comply with the loan agreement.

The Authorization is delivered to the lender along with the promissory note, security agreement, guaranty agreements, and settlement sheets required by the SBA to document the loan. Presented in a standard SBA format, the Authorization is informally organized into five parts:

Declarations - The first section declares the SBA's authorization and agreement to guaranty the lender's loan as specified, identifying the borrower, the amount of the loan, and the extent of the guaranty.

Documentation - The second section defines which SBA documents are required by the agency to enact this guaranteed transaction:

> • *SBA Note - Form 147* - The SBA requires the lender to use this form as the promissory note governing the transaction. A conformed copy of the note is sent back to the SBA along with the guaranty fee, which is defined in this section.

> • *SBA Settlement Sheet - Form 1050* - The SBA requires the lender to report each disbursement of loan proceeds on this form, which identifies to whom the loan proceeds are paid. This requirement insures that the loan is disbursed in consistence with the SBA approval of the loan.

> • *Compensation Agreements - Form 159* - The SBA requires the lender to submit this form for each party who received a professional fee for work related to the subject loan.

> • *Authorization* - The SBA requires the lender to obtain the borrower's signature of the Authorization and retain the original in the loan file.

Precedents - The third section usually defines four conditions to which the lender must affirm and comply in order to insure the SBA participation:

- The lender must acknowledge that the guaranty is subject to the provisions of the Guaranty Agreement between the SBA and the lender.

- The lender must acknowledge and agree to disburse the loan within a specified time frame, unless the SBA consents to extending that period.

- The lender must affirm that it has not received any evidence of unremedied adverse changes in the borrower's financial condition or status since the loan approval which would warrant withholding further disbursement of the loan.

- The lender affirms that the Authorization is subject to the representations made by the borrower, representations made by the lender, conditions set forth by the lender in its application for the guaranty, and conditions set forth in the Authorization.

Terms - The fourth section defines the specific terms under which the contemplated loan is to be enacted in order to qualify for the guaranty.

- *Repayment Terms* - The Authorization defines the exact repayment terms under which the loan is extended, including the following information:

    Repayment Period - The repayment term of the loan is defined, including the number of years in which repayment is to occur, and the number of installments expected in that period. The first payment date is also specified.

    Interest Rate - The interest rate of the loan is defined. If the rate is variable, the index by which the rate may be adjusted is explained, along with the time period in which such an adjustment may occur. Disclosure is made that, if the SBA repurchases its guaranteed portion of the loan in the event of default, the interest rate will be permanently fixed at the then current interest rate.

    Maturity - The maturity of the loan is defined as the length of time it takes for the loan to be paid in full. There are several variables that determine the maturity. For example, the lender is permitted to apply installment payments first to any outstanding interest and then to principal. This provision can significantly impact the repayment

146

of the loan in a situation where the borrower is frequently late in submitting payments.

The Authorization states that any unpaid principal and interest will be due at the date of the last scheduled installment, regardless of the amount of a normal installment. The borrower will also be liable for reimbursing the lender for any extraordinary costs incurred in administrating, collecting, or liquidating the loan at the time of the final payment.

A "due on sale" provision is contained in this section - it states that if the borrower transfers or encumbers any asset used as collateral for the loan without permission from the lender and the SBA, the maturity of the loan may be accelerated.

The lender is permitted to assess the borrower with a late penalty of five percent of the payment amount for any installment received more than ten days after that payment was due.

• *Use of Proceeds Limitations* - The Authorization specifies the exact allocation of loan proceeds as approved by the lender and the SBA, with the following provisions governing these distributions:

The lender is to distribute the funds whenever possible with joint payee checks issued to the borrower and the ultimate recipient of the proceeds.

The borrower must usually present documentation to substantiate the allocations, such as a contract, bill of sale, price quote, or invoice. If the borrower has been approved for working capital financing, the lender will expect an updated budget of where the proceeds will be allocated. These funds will be distributed directly to the borrower. If the borrower is refinancing another loan, the other lender will have to furnish a written payoff as of the date of closing.

Up to ten percent of the loan amount, to a maximum of $10,000, may be disbursed directly to borrower as working capital if the final budgeted allocation of loan proceeds and closing costs do not use the entire loan.

• *Collateral Requirements* - The Authorization will specify the exact assets which are to be used to secure the loan and will detail the conditions under which their encumbrance is expected. A variety of SBA security documents may be referred to, depending on the specific collateral offered by the borrower:

> *Security Agreement - Form 1059* - The borrower is required to execute this form to encumber personal property assets, and the Authorization should specify in which lien position the lender should be. If the lender is to be subordinated to a senior lender, the Authorization will note the name of the lender and the amount of the outstanding senior loan.

> The Authorization will also refer to use of the UCC-1 Financing Statement, which is a standard document for recording public notice of the lender's lien on the borrower's personal property assets. The lender will attach a detailed list of these assets (with serial numbers, if available) to the UCC-1 and will record this statement in the county where the property is located.

> *Deed to Secure Debt - RO IV 147* - The borrower is required to execute this form to encumber real property assets, and the Authorization should specify in which lien position the lender should be. If the lender is to be subordinated to a senior lender, the Authorization will note the name of the lender and the amount of the outstanding senior loan.

> *Guaranty - Form 148* - The borrower (or the individuals who own the borrowing entity) are required to execute this form, which provides for a joint and several personal guaranty of the loan. Provisions describing this requirement may or may not describe collateral, depending on the agreement the borrower has reached with the lender during negotiations.

> *Assignment of Life Insurance - RO IV Form 82* - The borrower (or the individuals who own the borrowing entity) are required to execute this form if there is a requirement to provide life insurance to secure the loan. A comparable form provided by the insurer may be substituted.

Lease Agreement - The borrower is required to submit a copy of the Lease Agreement (if the borrower occupied leased premises) to confirm that the remaining term of the lease is extended to a minimum of the length of the loan repayment period.

Lessor's Agreement - RO IV Form 77 - The borrower is required to obtain the execution of this agreement with the lessor. The Lessor's Agreement protects the lender from a landlord attempting to assert any interest in the borrower's personal assets or other assets in which the lender encumbers to secure the loan and which may be situated in the landlord's premises.

Collateral Assignment of Lease - RO IV Form 79 - If the borrower has been approved for financing using the Alter-Ego Concept, this form is required to provide the lender with an assignment of the lease on the business premises to the Alter-Ego. The Alter-Ego Concept is employed when assets are purchased in the name of the business owner and leased to the business entity, which also guarantees the loan.

• *Additional Real Estate Requirements* - There are an additional set of covenants and documents required if the lender is encumbering real estate collateral. These include:

Single Property Deed to Secure Debt - The lender is required to file a separate deed to secure debt for each parcel of real property taken as collateral.

Agreement as to Additional Advances - RO IV Form 26 - When the lender is taking a subordinate position on the borrower's real property, the lender will require the senior lender to execute this document. This form protects the lender from losing collateral coverage if a senior lender were to advance additional proceeds to the borrower under the senior loan agreement.

Title Insurance - The lender is required to obtain title insurance without any survey exceptions on real property parcels where the lender is to have a first priority lien. This requirement includes a current survey of the subject property to insure that there are no property encroachments or boundary errors.

Attorney's Certificate of Title - RO IV Form 37 - The lender is permitted to use a guaranteed title search for parcels where the lender is to be in a subordinated lien position.

Separate Guaranty - Each owner of title on a particular parcel of real property will be required to execute a separate guaranty, even if the title holder does not have a direct interest in the borrower.

Appraisal - The borrower is required to provide the lender with an appraisal that is not more than six months old that support the specific valuation used to obtain approval of the loan. If the appraisal determines that the property has a lower value, the borrower will have to provide additional equity or additional collateral, or the lender may reduce the loan.

Survey - The borrower is required to provide the lender with a current survey which shows the existing boundaries and improvements.

Minimum Occupancy - For existing buildings, the borrower is required to occupy at least 50% of the premises.

• *Additional Personal Property Requirements* - There are an additional set of covenants and documents required if the lender is encumbering personal property collateral. These include:

Schedule A - The lender will require that the borrower provide a detailed list of the personal property assets securing the loan. This list will be attached to the UCC-1 and the Security Agreement, both of which will contain language specifying that the property pledged will include but will not be limited to the items on Schedule A. Where applicable, all assets on Schedule A should be described with the manufacturer's name and the model and serial numbers.

Lien Search - The lender is required to conduct a lien search to evidence that the requisite lien position is acquired.

On-Site Inspection - The lender must certify to the SBA that an on-site inspection of the personal property asset was conducted prior to the first disbursements of the loan proceeds.

There may be other documentation required to perfect the borrower's collateral, depending on the exact nature, ownership, and location of the collateral assets.

Conditions and Covenants -   The fifth section sets forth several conditions with which the borrower must agree to comply during the term of the loan:

- *Execution* - The borrower must agree to execute all of the documents required (which are mentioned previously in this chapter).

- *Reimbursable Expenses* - The borrower agrees to reimburse the lender on demand for all expenses incurred for the borrower's application, and the making and administration of the loan. Most of these expenses will be charged to the borrower at the loan closing.

- *Books, Records, and Reports* - The borrower agrees to maintain records of business activities (including financial reports) and to provide them to the lender upon request. Further, the borrower agrees that the lender may inspect the financial records or appraise any asset of the business at any time.   The borrower also authorizes any municipal, state, or federal government authority to provide the lender or SBA with copies of information which may be on file about the borrower.

- *Management Consultants* - The borrower agrees not to engage the services of a management consultant without prior approval of the lender and the SBA.

- *Distributions and Compensation* - The borrower agrees to not make distributions of capital or assets, retire stock or partnership interests, consolidate or merge with another company, or make preferential arrangements with affiliated companies during the term of the loan. Further, the borrower will not provide any bonuses, distributions, gifts or loans to any owner, director, officer, or employee in any manner other than reasonable compensation for services during the term of the loan.

- *Hazard Insurance* - The borrower agrees to maintain hazard insurance on the fixed assets that are used to secure the loan. All insurance policies will name the lender as loss payee and/or mortgagor, as appropriate. The borrower's furniture, fixtures, and equipment must be insured to at least 90% of replacement cost.

Policies insuring buildings must include a mortgagor's clause indicating that the interest of the mortgagor shall not be invalidated by the neglect of the owner, and that the mortgagor will be given thirty days notice prior to cancellation. This clause is commonly referred to as the New York Standard Mortgage Clause.

- *Federal Taxes* - The borrower must insure that all federal withholding taxes are paid up-to-date and that there are no outstanding tax liens against the borrower.

- *Change of Ownership* - The borrower must agree not to change the ownership, control of the business, the business name, or the form of business organization, without the approval of the lender and the SBA.

- *Receipt of SBA Forms* - The borrower must execute the following SBA forms in compliance with federal regulations governing guaranteed loans:

> *Form 1624 - Certification Regarding Debarment* - This document is required to attest that the borrower, the individual, and the business entity have not been debarred from doing business with the federal government due to any administrative, disciplinary or other action specifically restricting the respective parties.

> *Form 652 - Assurance of Compliance For Nondiscrimination* - This document is required to attest that the borrower and any subsequent recipients of the SBA guaranteed loan proceeds agree to comply with SBA regulations pertaining to discrimination. These regulations require that no person be excluded from participation in, or be denied the benefits of, any federal financial assistance from the SBA based on age, color, handicap, marital status, national origin, race, religion, or sex.

- *Business Licenses* - The borrower is required to provide the lender with a copy of business licenses and any special operating permits or licenses required by the State.

• *Negative Pledge Covenant* - The borrower agrees not to encumber or convey any asset or ownership of the business without prior approval of the lender and the SBA.

• *Opinion of Counsel - ADO Form 20* - The lender's attorney is required to provide an opinion regarding the loan transaction.

• *Other Insurance* - Depending on the nature of the collateral provided by the borrower, additional insurance may be required:

> *Flood Insurance* - If the business or collateral is located in a special hazard area subject to flooding, mud slides, or erosion, the borrower must agree to maintain Federal Flood Insurance in the maximum amount available.

> *Automobile Insurance* - If motor vehicles are used as collateral, the borrower must agree to maintain collision and liability in an amount satisfactory to the lender, with the lender named as the loss payee.

• *Borrower's Equity* - Prior to the first disbursement of the loan, the borrower must provide satisfactory evidence of the requisite equity injection, as represented in the loan application.

• *Standby Agreement - Form 155* - Any subordinate creditors of the borrower must execute a Standby Agreement to subordinate the lien rights and other general rights in favor of the SBA lender.

• *Organizational Authority* - The borrower must substantiate its authority to enter into the loan by producing organizational documents providing such information:

> If the borrower is a corporation, it must provide:

>> Corporate Resolution - Form 160
>> Certificate of Good Standing
>> Articles of Incorporation
>> Qualification of foreign corporation to do business in the resident state, if applicable.

If the borrower is a partnership, it must provide:

Partnership Agreement
Certificate as to Partners - Form 160A
Certificate of Limited Partnership, if applicable
Certificate of Existence

• *Bulk-Sales Notice* - If applicable, the borrower must provide the lender with evidence of compliance with any applicable state or federal bulk-sales laws.

• *Building Compliance* - The borrower must provide evidence that any commercial buildings used as collateral conform to all applicable building, zoning, and sanitation codes, as well as the Americans With Disabilities Act of 1990, as amended.

• *Fixed Asset Limit* - If included, the borrower may agree to limit the acquisition of fixed assets to a particular level, subject to approval from the lender and the SBA.

• *Franchise Agreement* - The borrower must provide the lender with a copy of any franchise agreement to which it is a party.

• *Alien Registration* - If applicable, the borrower must provide the lender with a copy of the alien registration of any owners who are not U.S. citizens.

• *Environmental Assessment Conditions* - If the borrower is securing the loan with commercial property, the lender and the SBA will require that an environmental assessment of the property be obtained. The following conditions will be included in the Authorization:

Option to Modify or Cancel - The lender and SBA reserve the right to modify or cancel the loan if environmental contamination is discovered on the property.

Environmental Assessment - The lender and the SBA will require an Environmental Disclosure Form, an Environmental Questionnaire (ADO For 001), or a Phase 1 Environmental Audit.

154

The determination of which assessment is used is based on the historic use of the property and development in the immediate area.

UST Requirements - If the property contains underground storage tanks (USTs), the borrower is required to comply with all federal and state regulations for USTs. The borrower must also provide the lender with evidence on an annual basis of its compliance with these regulations, including the EPA financial responsibility regulations.

• *Alter Ego Concept* - If using an Alter Ego loan, the borrower must agree that the respective ownership in collateral assets and in the business entity will remain identical and in the same proportion until the loan is repaid, unless the lender and the SBA consent to any change.

• *Construction Loan Conditions* - If the borrower is using any portion of the loan proceeds to build a new structure or make improvements on an existing structure, the following provisions shall be in the Authorization:

Construction Documentation - The borrower will be required to provide the lender with the following documentation related to construction:

Building plans and specifications.

Evidence of Builder's Risk Insurance and Workers Compensation Insurance carried by the contractor.

Evidence that the contractor has furnished a performance bond for 100% of labor and materials, with the borrower and lender named as the obligees.

Agreement of Compliance - Form 601.

Construction Contract

Borrower's Equity - Evidence of the borrower's equity contribution toward the construction project must be provided, since the borrower's funds will be used before any loan proceeds will be advanced.

Survey - The borrower must furnish an as-built survey prior to any advances of the construction funds in order to show existing boundaries and improvements.

Earthquake Standards - For new buildings, the borrower must provide evidence that the project will meet the requirements of the "National Earthquake Hazards Reduction Program Recommended Provisions for the Development of Seismic Regulations for New Buildings." A certificate may be obtained from the project architect to fulfill this requirement.

Interim Inspections - As the borrower requests loan advances, the lender will conduct interim inspections of the project to verify that construction conforms to plans and specifications.

Retainage - The lender will withhold 10% of the construction contract proceeds until the project is completed.

Lien Waivers - The lender will require all contractors, subcontractors, and suppliers to sign a lien waiver prior to each loan disbursement.

Cost Overruns - If the borrower's project experiences cost overruns, the borrower or the lender must provide additional funds to complete the project.

Minimum Occupancy - For newly constructed buildings, the borrower is required to occupy at least 67% of the premises.

- *American-Made Products* - To the extent possible, the borrower agrees to purchase American-made equipment and products with the proceeds of the loan.

- *Lottery Income Restriction* - The borrower must acknowledge that the Authorization restricts the borrower to no more than 33% of annual gross revenue being generated from commissions on official state lottery sales.

Execution - The sixth section confirms the general legal conditions of the Authorization which the SBA, lender, and borrower must acknowledge. The three parties execute the Authorization in this section.

How Can the Borrower Close the Loan Faster?

Most borrowers are ready to close the loan within a week of the final loan approval, but it is very rare that the lender can be prepared in this time frame. There is a lot of work to prepare for a loan closing.

Rather than sit frustrated on the sidelines, the borrower can assist the lender and closing attorney with many tasks. This help will make a difference in the time required to complete the transaction.

Start Closing Before the Loan is Approved - Much of the due diligence required before closing is not conducted until after final approval of the loan, such as appraisals, surveys, and environmental assessments. This delay is due to the unwillingness of most borrowers to risk spending thousands of dollars on these studies without having the assurance that the loan will be approved.

One method to shorten the time gap between SBA loan approval and loan closing is to initiate these time-consuming activities earlier in the process. While this does jeopardize the borrower's funds, in many situations the risk is very low because of the borrower's clear financial qualification and SBA eligibility. The lender should be able to express some degree of confidence as to whether the borrower should take this risk.

If the borrower has the appraisal, survey, environmental assessment, life insurance, and even a title opinion and lien search in hand when the loan is approved, the loan could be closed in a matter of days.

Review the Authorization - The borrower should obtain a copy of the Authorization from the lender or the SBA as soon as possible and carefully review it. The borrower should determine that the document accurately reflects the transaction negotiated between the borrower and the lender.

The borrower should insure that it is capable of complying with the terms of the Authorization, and should inquire about any items which are not understood up front. If any modifications are needed, the borrower should bring these items to the attention of the lender immediately, since changes may require several weeks for approval.

Get Life Insurance! - If the Authorization requires the borrower to furnish life insurance on any of the individual owners or managers, application for these insurance policies should begin immediately. A $1 million life insurance policy can no longer be obtained over the telephone.

With the greater incidence of life threatening infections related to HIV, insurers are much more selective about issuing large policies, and most will require a blood test for even a $100,000 policy. Blood work requires time, and the underwriting of the insurer may also include financial qualification in order to justify the policy.

To evidence compliance with the insurance requirement, the borrower may be required to furnish an actual policy at the loan closing. The life insurance policy may take four to six weeks to issue. It is wise to apply for life insurance coverage as soon as possible during the loan closing stage.

Getting the Lender's Attention - When borrowers are anxious to close, they can expedite the time frame by facilitating the process. A borrower can help the lender and closing attorney by providing additional information or performing assignable tasks. A borrower who communicates directly, regularly, and constructively can shorten the time required to close.

Supplying Additional Documentation - The borrower may be required to produce additional material for the lender's attorney, primarily to document specific conditions and to provide further information about the collateral.

Even though some of this information may have been provided previously to the lender, it is easier for the borrower to reproduce it for the closing attorney. The attorney will be particularly concerned about preparation of the security documents and insuring compliance with the terms of the Authorization. The Authorization may involve documentation that was not required during the application stage. The borrower will need to produce this additional information for the closing attorney.

Monitoring the Professionals - Borrowers using real estate as collateral will be required to obtain assistance from professionals for preparation of an appraisal, survey, environmental assessment, and other information required by the lender's due diligence. These professionals may be very efficient in producing their reports, or they may hold up the entire closing. The borrower should get involved in this part of the process to insure that it moves as swiftly as possible.

The borrower should coordinate the work with these professionals as closely as possible. After determining who the lender has engaged for these matters, the borrower should contact them independently of the lender to schedule an appointment.

The borrower should make an effort to be present when the professional inspects the property. Often, the professional will have questions about the site or structure and, if no one is available, assumptions may be substituted for facts. The borrower's presence can enhance the report by supplying updated information which is usually more accurate and more detailed than would otherwise be available to the professional.

Putting Out the Fires - Problems frequently arise during the due diligence performed in preparation for loan closing. Maybe the borrower's appraisal came in too low, or some environmental contamination was discovered on the real property. Maybe an old, unsatisfied mortgage is found to be outstanding from a lender paid off ten years ago, and the property has been subsequently sold three times.

Often the lender or the lender's attorney will react to these problems as if the deal is off, as if the borrower is out of luck. But, usually the problem can be resolved and the transaction is far from dead. Of greater concern is getting the parties focused on resolving the problem without any unnecessary delay in closing the loan.

It is important for the borrower to determine as quickly as possible the exact nature of the problem and the remedy for solving it. The borrower should not rely strictly on the lender's attorney to define the resolution, because the lender's best solution is not always optimum for the borrower. The borrower should obtain the appropriate professional assistance in managing the resolution of the particular problem.

No one will make solving the problem a greater priority than the borrower. Instead of waiting for someone else to initiate the resolution, the borrower must manage the situation personally to make sure the loan closing is postponed for weeks instead of months.

If the problem is rather minor, the borrower may be able to continue with the closing on schedule by setting aside enough money in escrow to cover the maximum exposure to the problem. For example, if there is an outstanding mortgage for $3,000 which the borrower asserts has been satisfied, but the holder cannot be located immediately, the borrower can put $3,000 in escrow at closing to assure the lender that the mortgage will be satisfied.

How Can Closing Costs Be Reduced?

One of the most frequent complaints about SBA loans is the total cost involved to close the loan. Borrowers obtaining long-term real estate financing can expect to pay as much as six percent of the total loan to close. In reality many of these costs are simply inherent to the deal and cannot be avoided.

Accepting these closing expenses is a combination of putting the costs in perspective and determining which costs can be reduced or eliminated. The borrower can influence these costs in certain circumstances. The following paragraphs describe some of the common costs associated with closing an SBA loan and how the borrower might lower them in certain instances.

SBA Guaranty Fee - The lender must pay and usually requires the borrower's reimbursement of a fee to the SBA for the loan guaranty. This fee was raised in FY 1996 to the following scale:

Guaranteed Portion of Loan	Guaranty Fee
$0 - $80,000	2%
$80,000 - $250,000	3%
$250,001 - $500,000	3.5%
$500,001 - $750,000	3.875%

If the loan carries a 75% guaranty, the fee is calculated by multiplying the guaranteed portion of the loan by the appropriate fee. This fee is essentially the insurance premium to fund the agency's bad loan losses from its collective portfolio of guaranteed loans.

The only way to reduce this fee is to be fortunate enough to be in a competitive situation between two lenders. If both lenders want to make the business loan, the borrower could negotiate to have one of the lenders absorb all or part of the SBA guaranty fee. This option is available only to the strongest borrowers who are highly qualified financially.

Attorney's Fees - The SBA loan is always closed by an attorney due to the complexities involved in complying with the Authorization. Lenders would simply invite too much exposure not to involve a professional for this task. And, of course, the cost of the attorneys will be passed on to the borrower.

Depending on the dynamics of the transaction, attorneys will have varying degrees of involvement. If there is real property included, the attorneys will have more responsibilities in the closing and the costs will be proportionately greater.

Attorney's fees will vary greatly depending on the locale, the local market, the size of the firm, and the firm's familiarity with SBA loans. These fees may range from a flat $1,500 up to roughly 1% of the transaction plus title insurance.

The borrower can reduce the attorney's fees in several ways:

- The borrower can ask the lender to select a firm with lower costs. Understanding that the borrower is sensitive to the closing costs, the loan officer may have some latitude to influence which firm is selected and to request a lower fee.

- The borrower can ask the loan officer to select an attorney who has previously worked for the borrower. If the attorney does not have a conflict of interest, the familiarity with the borrower may reduce the costs of the transaction, even though the attorney will now represent the lender.

- The borrower can ask the attorney for a written fee estimate. Before any work begins, therefore the borrower can discuss the level of the estimate with the lender and the attorney. Attorneys, like other professionals, find it easier to charge higher fees once the work has been performed. When seeking the business, they seem to be a little more reasonable on fees, particularly when required to provide a quote up-front.

- If certain legal work has been done in the past couple of years which relates to the loan or the collateral (such as title examinations), the borrower can provide this information to the attorney. If the borrower's real property has title insurance, the attorney may be able to renew the old title policy and conduct a shorter title search. This combination should significantly reduce a portion of the legal fees involved.

• The borrower may be able to provide some of the clerical work for the attorney, thereby reducing the add-on cost associated with a loan closing. For example, because the attorney must assemble several closing packages, the borrower saves money by providing several copies of the necessary documents. The borrower can reproduce them less expensively than the attorney.

Other Professional Fees - The borrower will have to bear the costs of several professionals involved in the due diligence phase of closing the loan. Such specialist as an appraiser, environmental engineer, surveyor, and construction inspector may be involved to provide independent opinions for the specific transaction.

Fees for these specialists may range from $750 to $4,000 each, depending on the situation, the specific nature of their engagement, and the local market in which they work. The best way to manage these fees are as follows:

• The borrower can ask the lender to select a professional with lower costs. Understanding that the borrower is sensitive to these costs, the loan officer may have some latitude to influence which firm is selected and to request that the professional negotiate a lower fee.

• The borrower can ask the loan officer to select an professional who has previously worked for the borrower. If these professionals are familiar with the borrower or the borrower's assets, this fact may reduce the costs of the transaction, even though they are now representing the lender. In the case of a surveyor, appraiser, or environmental engineer, the lender should be able to accept an update of the previous work performed..

• The borrower can ask the professional for a written fee estimate. Before any work begins, therefore the borrower can discuss the level of the estimate with the lender and the professional. Specialist find it easier to charge higher fees once the work has been performed. When seeking the engagement, they seem to be a little more reasonable on fees, particularly when required to provide a quote up-front.

- If certain work has been done in the past couple of years for the borrower which relates to the collateral (such as appraisals or environmental reports), the borrower can provide this information to the specialist. This information could significantly reduce the professional fees involved.

- If appropriate, the borrower can ask that the lender to limit the scope of the professional's engagement to the exact information required by the Authorization. Often, the professional's report includes information not requested or required, which can lead to higher fees for the borrower.

Recording Costs and Taxes - Many counties and states assess fees for the recordation of certain documents required to perfect the lender's lien on the borrower's collateral assets, such as mortgages and UCC-1s. These fees vary greatly from state to state, but usually must be considered the cost of doing business. They are certainly not negotiable, and the lender will typically not absorb them.

Prepaid Interest - Depending on when the loan is closed, the borrower will be responsible for a varying sum of prepaid interest. SBA loans are placed on a standardized repayment schedule, which calls for the first loan payment to be due on the first day of the second month after the loan closes.

For example, if a loan closes on the fifteenth day of January, the first payment will be due on March 1. However, since interest is billed in arrears (payable for the period preceding the payment), the interest collected on the March 1 payment would be for the period February 1 through March 1. Therefore, at the loan closing, the lender would collect a prepaid interest charge for the period from January 15 through January 31. This prepaid interest is in lieu of a payment being due on February 1 - on larger loans, the prepaid interest can significantly alter the cash disbursed at loan closing. Borrowers can lower this sum by closing the loan as close as possible to the last day of the month.

It is important for the borrower to put the costs of closing a loan in perspective. In reality, these costs are a necessary part of borrowing money and simply cannot be avoided. The borrower should view the costs over the life of the loan, rather than simply in the period in which they are incurred. If the borrower is obtaining a $1,000,000 real estate loan for twenty-five years, the $40,000 in closing costs equate to only $1,600 per year.

Chapter 7

Other Borrower Issues

Should the Borrower Use a Loan Packager?

Many small business owners seeking financing have recognized the value of using professional advice. But just as many business people have become victims of unscrupulous or inept loan brokers - loan brokers who either waste valuable time conducting a hopeless search for capital or who collect fees which are undeserved and never earned.

Loan consultants play an important role in today's banking environment. With the consolidation of thousands of banks and the introduction of many of new financing venues, entrepreneurs cannot be expected to keep track of the constantly changing financial marketplace.

Fortunately, there are many consultants whose primary efforts are focused on the SBA loan market. These consultants, often referred to as "packagers," are positioned to provide small businesses with the expertise of how and where to access SBA financing. The value of these services is generally in proportion to what they cost.

Any consultant willing to work on behalf of the borrower for several months without a retainer purely on a contingency basis, is usually worth everything paid to them - nothing. Because borrowers can be fickle, seasoned consultants will not make large time investments without tangible commitments on the part of clients in form of monetary deposits. These consultants have successfully raised many millions in loans for borrowers who changed their minds, resulting in no compensation for the considerable effort.

Before writing a check to engage these consultants, the borrower should take the time to validate their capabilities in successfully obtaining loans. Does their track record match their confidence about how well they will accomplish their mission? This short exercise could save the borrower from an expensive and frustrating exercise in futility.

First, the borrower should request a list of references from the consultant. In contacting these businesses which engaged the services of this consultant, the borrower can determine how well the consultant performed. Did the business obtain the financing it needed? If not, why? If so, was the time frame reasonable? Did the consultant communicate with the business on a regular and informed basis? Did the consultant have a firm grasp of the company's objectives, and were those objectives met due to the efforts of the consultant?

The borrower can then ask the consultant for references in the lending community. Obviously, the consultant will not permit the borrower to contact any potential lender which may be the target of the loan proposal. But the borrower can speak with other lenders, outside the scope of the proposed deal, to which the consultant has referred transactions.

What was the lender's attitude toward the consultant? Does the lender rely on the consultant merely for referrals, or does the lender express confidence in the consultant's ability to analyze potential deals? In other words, does the consultant's opinion count, or is the consultant only throwing darts at the wall with the borrower's deal.

Finally, the borrower should determine whether the consultant is a member of any trade associations, such as the Chamber of Commerce, the National Federation of Independent Businesses, the National Association of Government Guaranteed Lenders, or other groups which support small businesses. These memberships are not necessarily a qualification, but they can be indicative of the success and standing of the consultant in the industry. These groups rarely provide references, but the borrower can verify the claimed membership status of the consultant.

The borrower should remember that the consultant is not the decision-maker for the loan request. Rather the consultant prepares the application and helps structure the transaction. But after selecting the lender and presenting the case, the consultant loses control of the timing and decision involved.

Most lenders commonly disregard the time constraints of their customers. If the loan needs to be reviewed by a government guarantor, such as the SBA, the lender also loses control of the deal. Everyone is in a hurry. As long as the consultant demonstrates diligence in performing specific responsibilities, the consultant should not be blamed for the action of others.

These consultants are business people, too. It is not unreasonable, therefore, for consultants to request the borrower to engage their services with a written agreement, and to require a retainer as an expression of commitment on the borrower's part. Services and advice cannot be repossessed, and the consultant should not be penalized for changes in the borrower's situation or strategy which render those services and advice useless.

To be cautious, the borrower should understand and agree to the compensation expectations of the consultant before work begins on the borrower's behalf. The consultant's willingness to work on a contingency may sound like a good arrangement for the borrower, but it also may indicate that the borrower is employing an inexperienced party to work on the loan application. Borrowers should beware of people who can make a living collecting $250 application fees.

A reasonable consultant will not ask for a retainer unless confident about successfully completing the borrower's deal. The prospects of obtaining a loan cannot be reliably predicted without a thorough review of the borrower's financial statements and other pertinent data.

Loan consultants can easily create value for a business; they allow the borrower to concentrate on the company rather that hopping through twenty banks, leaving a track record on the owner's credit report for every lender which turned down the deal. But borrowers should be willing to pay for quality services and should know who is engaged for this important assignment.

How Should the Borrower Use Its Attorney?

Many borrowers utilize legal counsel for a variety of business affairs, and naturally want them involved in closing the SBA loan. Although there is nothing wrong with this procedure, it may prove to be an expensive duplication of efforts.

What the borrower's attorney can provide to the process is to review the documents the borrower is required to execute in order to obtain the loan and to fulfill the requirements of the lender and the SBA. That review can insure that someone representing the borrower's interest interprets these documents and understands the obligations.

What the borrower's attorney has very little chance of doing is to make many meaningful changes in the documentation for the borrower's benefit. The principal documentation used for SBA guaranteed loans is provided by the SBA and cannot be altered. These guaranteed loans are similar to federally insured housing loans. The standardization of documentation is necessary since these loans are eligible to be sold in a secondary market by the lender.

The borrowers attorney can function effectively by reviewing the Loan Authorization and Agreement. This document sets forth the terms under which the loan is being extended, and refers to the other documentation which is necessary. From this information, the borrower's attorney can determine the nature of the deal, clarify what is being required of the borrower in terms of repayment and collateral, and describe the consequences of default.

Dispelling Common Myths About the SBA

Thousands of businesses have avoided seeking assistance from the SBA due to a number of misconceptions about the agency. Professionals serving the market often spend time convincing qualified borrowers that participation is worth the effort, and that nothing terrible would happen to the business if the SBA guaranteed the debt. Of course, the paperwork is at times overwhelming, but so is an unguaranteed. This section addresses many of the most common and misleading myths.

The SBA Program Is Primarily for Women and Minorities - This myth is not true. The SBA guaranty programs are available for participation by all persons, regardless of race, color, creed, age, or ethnicity. In FY 1994, 65% of all SBA loan guarantees were made for white males.

The Agency does employ a relatively new initiative to encourage women and minority borrowers to utilize the program. These borrower categories are permitted to be pre-approved for loan guarantees before a lender has formally approved their loan requests. However, the agency does not provide any special funding allocations for these categories. Nor do women or minority participants receive any special consideration or credit-scoring which would provide agency assistance in a situation in which other borrowers would be denied.

Anybody Can Get an SBA Loan - There are limits. Participation with the SBA guaranty program is restricted to borrowers who qualify under certain conditions, relating to the size of the small business concern (in terms of revenues, net income, net worth, or number of employees, depending on the type of loan guaranty and the industry involved) and the nature of the business activity.

Borrowers seeking to benefit under the 7(a) guaranty program are restricted by either gross revenues of $5.0 million (with some exceptions based on the industry of the borrower) or limited by 500 employees in some specific industries which are labor intensive, such as manufacturing. Questions of eligibility can be directed to the Agency for clarification about specific situations.

Borrowers seeking to get assistance under the 504 Development Program are restricted by their average net income over the past three years (no more than $2.0 million annually, including affiliates) and net worth (no more than $6.0 million, including affiliates).

Businesses involved in real estate development, lending activities, gambling, and illegal activities are prohibited from receiving assistance from the loan guaranty program.

The Government Will Monitor the Business - Fears of "Big Brother" cause many small businesses to hesitate about the SBA guaranty program. Participation with the SBA includes no monitoring of the borrower's business activities, no government audits, and no inter-agency communications about the business operations.

The SBA does not have the interest, personnel, or mandate to provide any extraordinary supervision of the business unless the borrower is in default of the loan. When the borrower is in default, the SBA's interest will be strictly focused on working with the lender to recover the loan.

Obtaining SBA assistance does not increase the borrower's chances of being audited by the IRS or being examined by the OSHA, EPA, The Corps of Engineers, or any other government agency which regulates the operations of business and industry.

The Lender Does Not Care How Good or Bad the Business Is -This myth is totally false. Lenders participating with the SBA guaranty programs are responsible for making good loans. The SBA guaranty is intended to enhance a loan, not subsidize the bank to build a bad loan portfolio.

An unguaranteed portion of every loan will expose the lender to the full risk of the credit, and that portion is likely to increase in the next few years as funding for this program is restricted. Collecting bad loans can be very expensive in terms of time and money.

Do Affiliated Companies Affect the Application?

Affiliated companies affect the borrower's participation in the SBA loan guaranty programs by enlarging the parameters by which the lender has to determine eligibility for participation. Affiliates are defined as any other business entity in which at least a 20% interest is owned by the borrower, or any owner of at least 20% of the borrower . The affiliated companies are considered collectively with the enterprise for which the borrower is seeking to finance, for purposes of determining whether the subject company seeking financing is eligible under the program limitations.

That is, any and all business interests in which the borrower and any owners of the borrower, individually or collectively, own at least a 20% stake, are considered together with the entity seeking to borrow money. This composite is used to calculate the total sales, number of employees, net income, or net worth in determining the eligibility limitations for obtaining a loan guaranty.

The lender is required to confirm the borrower's eligibility if any affiliated companies exist. The borrower, therefore, should be prepared to provide the lender with financial information about the affiliated entities in order to allow assessment of eligibility. This financial documentation has to be provided to the SBA as well.

The Value of Relationship Banking

If the lender is a bank, the borrower should be sensitive to the fact that the bank is in the business of providing many more services than commercial loans. In fact banks are currently seeking to expand their list of services beyond the traditional services of money management and money handling and to enter into securities and insurance.

Banks need deposits with which to make loans. It is not important from where they get these deposits, and even whether they are time or demand deposits. Each day, banks need millions of dollars on deposit to meet their demands for cash to cover loans and withdrawals. Recognizing this aspect of the banking business, the borrower should be prepared to be confronted with a request or requirement to utilize the bank's depository services if the business loan is extended.

Relationship banking can have many positive features, and it is important to know the dynamics so that the borrower receives every advantage available. While the lending personnel are traditionally recognized as the bankers with significant influence in the business, the borrower should be aware that there are many other persons who are worthwhile to know.

In measuring a banking relationship, there are many services which a business may purchase:

Demand Deposit Account (DDA) - Virtually every person and certainly every commercial business maintains a demand deposit account or checking account. These are funds which the depositor places into an account to avoid having to manage large or frequent sums of cash. These funds are withdrawn upon the depositor's "demand," a directive issued in the form of a written check.

Time Deposits (TD) - These accounts are placed on deposit with a bank for a definite or indefinite amount of time. The bank pays the depositor interest on these funds, the amount of which varies according to how long the depositor agrees to leave the funds in the account. There are a variety of time deposit accounts, including savings accounts and certificates of deposit, all of which have specific features and benefits.

Safe Deposit Boxes - Banks provide safe deposit boxes within their vault for storage of a depositor's valuable assets or documents.

Merchant Credit Services - Every retail business which accepts Master Card, Visa, American Express, or Discover Cards has to have a merchant account through which to clear these charges. These accounts are provided on a qualified basis, dependent on confirmation of the merchant's business operation and financial stability.

Credit - The best known service provided by banks is credit. There are more types of loans available than ever before, with banks using a variety of credit products to deliver funds to consumers for short, intermediate and long-term reasons. Many banks make car loans, issue credit cards, and handle home loans.

The point of discussing these other services is to suggest that business borrowers should use their demand for these services as an attribute when requesting a commercial loan. If the borrower can demonstrate to the lender that the accommodation of credit will also provide the bank with a substantive customer for other services, the lender may be persuaded to stretch in some ways to approve the loan request. A combination of a few of these accounts can mean thousands of dollars in fee income to the bank, and provide a new source of inexpensive deposits for them.

In summarizing all of the services used, personally and in business, the borrower represents an impressive opportunity for the bank. Other shareholders, partners, and even senior managers can be included when the borrower compiles a list of potential business available to the bank.

The prospect of these other relationship accounts will not make a bad loan proposal good, but it can certainly enhance a questionable deal - and provide the lender with incentives to give the borrower a chance. If the borrower does not need this kind of assistance for loan approval, the relationship accounts may help improve the interest rate or other terms offered on the loan by the bank.

Chapter 8

What If the Lender Says *NO*?

How to Handle Rejection

Sometimes the lender says *no* - maybe even without conditions, exceptions, or encouragement, maybe even without a phone call or a letter. Regardless of how positive the discussions have been, how upbeat the loan officer is about the borrower's prospects, and how much the loan officer wants to say *yes*, the borrower's application is subject to denial.

Many lending personnel expose their distance from the decision-making process, or their own inexperience, by continually encouraging the borrower about the prospects of approval up through the last minute. But when the committee says *no*, the loan officer can find all sorts of things that are wrong with the proposed deal. This scenario goes back to the weaknesses in the loan approval process discussed earlier.

No is one half of the possible replies available to the lender to respond to a loan request. The borrower should listen carefully to the *no* to understand the different ways it may have been said. An astute borrower will listen carefully to the explanation spoken by the lender after the word *because*.

172

The lender makes a decision based on business, not on personality. The lender is responsible for making a decision based on qualifying the loan request within the parameters that must be maintained.

The borrower should not: get mad, become defensive, be hurt, feel betrayed, or say anything that may irreparably damage future opportunities to obtain financing from this lender. Perhaps the loan officer has a difficult time being blunt; perhaps the loan officer is matter-of-fact about the unwillingness of the institution to provide the loan; or perhaps the loan officer feels uneasy about communicating the disappointing news.

No matter how well or how badly the lender delivers the answer to the borrower, and regardless of how well or how badly the borrower handles the news, it is important for the borrower to keep a positive demeanor and be very cordial. The borrower needs the loan officer's assistance in understand the reasoning behind the lender's rejection. That assistance will not be forthcoming if the borrower creates an uncomfortable situation after being turned down.

How Did the Loan Officer Say NO?

There are many ways in which a lender can say *no*. Listening to and analyzing the negative reply to the loan request is the next step in the loan application process. It is what the loan officer says that is important: the explanation, the details, the analysis of the borrower's position. How does the lender said *no*?

"No, but..." - Perhaps the lender provides the borrower with ways to change the request in order to provide the lender with a way to say *yes*. Often, borrowers only hear the word *no*, and miss the lender's request to hear the word *please*.

"No, unless..." - Maybe the lender gave the borrower a conditional *no*, which could be changed if the borrower were to meet specified conditions or agree to more restrictive terms.

"I cannot say yes because..." - Sometimes the lender does not say *no* at all, but also does not say *yes*. Listening can sometimes tell the borrower how to overcome the lender's specific reservations in order to get the final *yes*.

"Not yet..." - Maybe the borrower has submitted the request too early. Is the lender not yet comfortable with the level of success of the business? Is it too early for substantive trends to justify the borrower's ambition to expand? Sometimes the lender is actually saying *wait.*

"No, because the borrower..." - Maybe lenders turn down requests because of specific objections or reservations that they cannot overcome. Identifying these problems will assist the borrower in re-focusing the loan request at a later date or submitting it to another lender.

"No, because the lender..." - Sometimes the restrictions of the institution will not allow a lender to say *yes.* Maybe the request is outside the lender's market area, or greater than the lending limit. If the lender's answer to the loan request is *no* because of what they cannot or will not do, the borrower can be encouraged that the request is valid. The borrower can probably find another lender to agree with the request.

"Hell no..." - Sometimes a blunt *no* should cause the borrower to reflect inward as to the validity of the proposal. Is it realistic that any lender will be able to extend the financing? Negative replies without explanations sometimes indicate fundamental weaknesses in the proposal. The borrower can use a negative response constructively for redesigning the business plan.

There are as many variations of saying "*no*" as there are people and situations. It is not the answer the borrower is seeking, but neither is it invaluable or irreversible. Listening to the loan rejection is the key to learning how to get the proposal approved.

What is the Next Step?

There are many ways to respond to a loan denial. Selecting the correct response will be integral to getting approval the next time the borrower presents the proposal. Determining the next step requires that the borrower fully understand how and why the lender turned the application down.

As mentioned earlier, it is imperative to listen to the lender's explanation without an emotional response to cloud the borrower's understanding. Without putting the lend on the defensive, the borrower should ask questions. Respectful inquiries and specific answers will benefit the borrower in making the proposal succeed at a later date.

Several days later, the borrower can call the lender to request an appointment for additional information about why the loan was rejected. The purpose of this meeting is for the borrower to learn by seeking answers from someone with a degree of expertise. These discussions are not intended to change the lender's mind about the proposed transaction, but rather to prepare the borrower for the next lender.

In preparing for this interview, the borrower should focus on business issues rather than personal reactions. By encouraging the lender to respond with directness, the borrower can create an opportunity for instructive commentary.

From the lender's perspective, what factors about the business were not acceptable: the industry, location, products, employees, capitalization, track record, deal, or even management? What weaknesses need to be addressed in the business for the next loan proposal?

Was the negative reply due to the lender? Often lenders steer away from particular loans because of a previous bad experience in the industry or because of the type of loan. Maybe the lender's loan policies, market area, or lending limits restrict participation in the borrower's request. Often, loan officers do not think in terms of what can be done, but rather in terms of what cannot be done. The burden of asking the right question is usually left with the borrower, who must determine on what basis the loan officer will respond affirmatively.

Was the lender's rejection intended to be permanent, or can conditions or specific benchmarks change the response? Will the lender ever consider this financing? If so, exactly what changes or conditions are required? Where is the lender's level of comfort, and can the borrower attain it? This information will give the borrower more parameters in which to react and make future choices.

Maybe the lender is telling the borrower to move on to the next lender. In this case, this lender can make recommendations about where else to apply. The borrower can ask why the proposal may be acceptable somewhere else; the answer will help the borrower know how the next lender should be approached.

Responding to the Lender's Objections

Identifying the qualifications, exceptions, alterations, and finality of the lender's rejection helps the borrower to determine why the lender said *no*. The following list includes some of the most common reasons for rejecting a loan request and some logical responses for the borrower:

Objection 1: *The business is under-capitalized.*

Lenders want the borrower to have either contributed or earned a substantive portion of the net worth of the business. In comparing the total debt to the total equity, there should be some measurable part of the company's financing provided from a source other than the lender.

Response: The borrower can take a number of measures to increase equity in the business:

- The borrower can inject more money into the company from such sources as savings, a second mortgage on an owner's home, liquidated investments, and the cash surrender value of a life insurance policies.

- The borrower can convert any subordinated debt or notes payable to the company to equity. Although this act may have consequences if and when the holders want to withdraw the money, it may be necessary to convince the lender of the borrower's commitment to the success of the business.

- The borrower can reduce any other liabilities of the company to a reasonable extent, at a discount if possible. Lowering the debt leverage can permit lenders to have a stronger position, without other liabilities distracting from their ability to be repaid.

- If the borrower does not have additional capital to contribute, maybe relatives, friends, employees or suppliers are willing to invest in the business. This additional capital could be structured to insure their priority in redemption as soon as the business accumulated additional capital to satisfy the requirements of the lender.

Objection 2: *The business has not earned money yet.*

Lenders expect that the borrower can support the business strategy with a track record of business success. If the company has perpetually lost money, most lenders may reason that additional financing will compound those losses and the borrower will be unable to repay the borrowed funds.

Response: The borrower's explanation of the financial history of the business (suggested earlier in the book) was not sufficient or was not reasonable. If the business has failed to profit, it is important to demonstrate why and to explain how the borrower will correct the problem.

Sometimes the borrower's strategy to earn profits is as simple as acquiring more efficient assets to achieve profitability. Lenders can usually accept this strategy if the borrower can prove that increases in productivity will indeed provide profits.

Sometimes, however, the strategy may be as vague as projecting additional expenditures on advertising and marketing. Lenders are less comfortable about financing this strategy since there are so many undefined and poorly understood variables which can cause failure.

The borrower should provide candid and detailed documentation explaining the periods in which a profit was not earned. In comparing those loss periods to periods in which the business did earn profits, the borrower can explain how the operations may have been different. Then the borrower should explain how the loan proceeds will be used to position the enterprise in a manner which can return or deliver profits to the business.

Objection 3: *The proposed loan is too much money.*

Lenders try to minimize loan requests by either reducing the marginal funds or trying to force the borrower to spend less in a particular part of the proposal. Their intent is to control their exposure and perhaps get the loan balance down as a percentage of the collateral.

Response: Only the borrower can decide if the business strategy can be achieved with a lower amount of funding. And, typically, only the borrower will know how much extra financial padding, incorporated into the request, can be lowered and not affect the business.

The borrower's response has to be based on how much money is actually needed and how an expenditure can be reduced without having a negative impact on the business plans. Alternatively, offering to provide additional collateral may cause the lender to reconsider the restriction, since the borrower has reduced the lender's perceived risk in the transaction.

Objection 4: *The business strategy is not sound.*

Loan officers will test the borrower's ideas against their collective experience (or inexperience) to evaluate whether the business has a reasonable chance of succeeding. If loan officers have strong reservations about the borrower's prospects, they will not provide financing.

Response: Lenders are not always correct - and they are almost always conservative. Maybe the borrower did not explain the business concept sufficiently to the loan officer, or maybe the loan officer has an incorrect or incomplete understanding of exactly what the borrower plans to accomplish.

The borrower should review the business strategy carefully, making sure that it fully describes each detail of the concept. These ideas can be supported with the articles, surveys, marketing studies, demographics, that influenced, inspired, or convinced the borrower to undertake this strategy.

Objection 5: *The business is too risky.*

Lenders exclude some industries from their lending market because the real or perceived risks inherent in those businesses are beyond the acceptable parameters of the lender. These exclusions may apply only to the local lender, or they may be fairly common among most lenders, depending on the industry within which the borrower operates.

Response: Perhaps the borrower has not effectively communicated how some of the risks can be counterbalanced. Depending on the locale and nature of the industry, the lender which may not want to finance the business may be the only lender which can.

Therefore the borrower has to convince the lender that the risks can be eliminated or limited. For example, by accepting tighter terms or providing sufficient collateral, the borrower can structure the transaction to protect the lender from exposure to costly servicing or potential loan losses.

Objection 6: *There is not enough collateral.*

This objection is probably the one most often used by lenders to turn down a loan. The lender wants a minimum of 1:1 collateral coverage, based on a discounted valuation of that collateral. Usually lenders will use their leverage to encumber virtually every asset the borrower has, even if those additional assets contribute little or no value as collateral to secure the loan.

The quantity and sufficiency of the collateral can overcome many objections, because lenders are usually too glad to rent the borrower its own money, even when that money may be tied up in other assets which can be encumbered for liquidation should the loan not be repaid.

Response: The borrower's response should be based on an honest recognition of the true value of the collateral. How much would it be worth in liquidation? Lenders are inclined to sell off repossessed assets grossly under market, seeking merely to recover their loan balance rather than getting the full value of the assets.

The borrower must learn about the market for selling assets similar to those offered as collateral. For example, a ten year old lathe which cost $5,000 has a discounted value for the lender. The borrower should pay for an appraisal from a used equipment dealer or equipment auctioneer. The dealer can quickly assess what the equipment would bring in a timely sale or in an auction. This information is germane to determining the leverage the lender will give the borrower on those assets.

Real estate assets also have to be valued, based on appraisals. The lender will typically advance a standard amount of the market value, thereby providing a margin for the lender to cover the time and associated cost of selling the property.

If the lender has not valued the collateral adequately, the borrower can provide additional information to prove the value. The borrower can challenge the lender's assessments only when a different value can be documented. When asked to review their reasoning, lenders can at least recognize a compromise value based on the evidence produced by the borrower.

If the assets are insufficient, the borrowers should offer to provide more collateral. Sometimes there are creative solutions to obtaining collateral value from assets which cannot be pledged. The borrower should review personal and business financial statements carefully, searching for a way to assign values to the lender.

In the absence of such collateral, the borrower can seek assistance from relatives, friends, associates, or investors who might be willing to hypothecate personal assets to the lender in order to secure the loan. In effect, these third parties would be providing a limited guaranty for the loan, only to the extent of their ownership in the assets they would agree to use as collateral for the loan.

Objection 7: *The financial projections are unreliable.*

Lenders will pay particular attention to the financial projections of the proposal to determine exactly how the borrower intends to repay the loan. Based on contributing factors, the loan officer does not always agree with the conclusions about revenue production or the cost of operations. If the loan officer does not accept the projections, the borrower's ability to service the debt becomes questionable.

Response: The borrower should examine the projections carefully and insure that the expectations have been adequately communicated. Reviewing the data or historical figures on which these projections have been based, the borrower should insure that this evidence is documented in the footnotes of the pro forma.

The borrower may need to make modifications to correct an error discovered by the lender or to revise the calculations. When comparing the new numbers against the debt service to pay back the loan, the borrower can determine if the deal is still feasible.

When confident with the numbers, the borrower should present them again with a line-by-line discussion (as necessary) to convince the loan officer of the soundness of these expectations. Determining the basis of the loan officer's questions or doubts, the borrower can attempt to validate those specific entries thoroughly.

The borrower's response to any of these objections does not guaranty that the lender will change the decision, but it is the logical step to take after the loan has initially been rejected. Since considerable effort has been invested in educating this lender about the company, the borrower should try to address these concerns before completely starting over with a new proposal to a new lender.

Keep Improving the Proposal

The burden to convince lenders to change the decision is on the borrower. Lenders are responsible only for evaluating the information put before them. In fact, after a decision has been made, it can be more difficult to persuade someone to change it. But if the loan officer is candid about what influenced the decision, the borrower may be able to challenge and overcome these objections. The loan could be approved quicker on reconsideration than if the borrower started over with a new lender, not understanding why the first lender denied the loan.

While the borrower is pursuing financing, it is important to continue updating the proposal with fresh information as it is available or as it is acquired. The company is completing a financial period every thirty days, and the financial information provided to the lender must be constantly updated to include the latest information.

If the borrower comes across pertinent information about the business, industry, or strategy to support the thesis of the proposal, the application should be updated with this information. Even if the proposal has already been submitted to the lender, the borrower should send the additional information for review.

Every sixty to ninety days (if the search for financing lasts for such a period), the borrower should review the entire plan from beginning to end. The proposal needs to be edited for updated information, corrections, and consistency. During the review process, the borrower can take advantage of any information or ideas obtained from a lender that turned down the request. By constantly polishing the proposal, the borrower can improve the chances of success.

There Are Other Lenders

Borrowers often lose sight that there are literally thousands of lenders. Given the commodity nature of SBA lending, the borrower has access not only to the local banks, but also to several non-bank lenders making SBA loans into any state.

Within these thousands of lenders, there are even more loan officers. Many of them will be less experienced in business than the borrower, and will be making decisions based on a limited career. Just because a loan officer reaches a certain conclusion does not mean it is correct. If the borrower feels confident about the merits of the loan proposal, one lender's negative reply should not prevent the plan from being presented to another lender.

Different lenders have different loan appetites, different expertise, even different levels of acceptable risks. The borrower should keep searching until finding the right lender which understands the business and feels comfortable with the management. These lenders are out there; they are sometimes just harder to find.

Sometimes the Borrower Will Not Qualify

The final answer may be that the business does not qualify for the loan it seeks - not only with the lender which rejected the loan, but with any lender. If the loan is turned down more than three times, there may be an inherent weakness preventing approval from any source. If this is the case, the borrower may need assistance from someone who can objectively evaluate the situation and the financing. Whether turning to a business consultant, CPA, or lender, the borrower should be able to rely on their direct experience and meaningful advice.

Sometimes there are other ways to accomplish the borrower's objectives than with a loan. Financing is not restricted to borrowing money, but can include such diverse options as selling part of the business, franchising, or bartering. All of these are other ways to exchange value owned for value needed.

Sometimes the borrower can reduce the loan by financing part of the transaction in another way. Although there are many possibilities, most of them may be more difficult, more expensive, and more time-consuming. But if the borrower wants the financing, it may have has to be taken in the manner in which it is available.

Maybe the borrower has tried to obtain financing prematurely. Perhaps another six, twelve, or eighteen months would improve the chances of approval by demonstrating the validity of the business strategy or other measurements of financial success.

The borrower should recognize that time is a good investment which can be healthy for the business. It may not satisfy ambition, but it may allow the borrower to obtain the financing from a position of strength. The established and stable record of a business decreases the lender's exposure, as well as the risk to the borrower.